EASY VISUALS FOR ENGLISH LANGUAGE TEACHERS

How to Make and Use Them

Richard Romo   **Boone Brinson**

National Textbook Company
NTC a division of *NTC Publishing Group* • Lincolnwood, Illinois USA

With special thanks to Julie Kniveton for her collaboration on this project.
Cover design by Nick Panos.

This edition first published in 1995 by National Textbook Company,
a division of NTC Publishing Group, 4255 West Touhy Avenue,
Lincolnwood (Chicago), Illinois 60646-1975 U.S.A.
Text © 1993 by Richard Romo and Boone Brinson.
Editorial, design, and layout © 1993 Editorial DELTI
Manufactured in the United States of America.

4 5 6 7 8 9 ML 9 8 7 6 5 4 3 2 1

CONTENTS

———DEDICATION———

We dedicate this book to Diane Hernández
because she had the faith that we could do it.

PREFACE

We began developing the ideas for this book while teaching at the Instituto Mexicano Norteamericano de Relaciones Culturales in Mexico City. We found ourselves in a situation with large classes, crowded conditions, long working hours and a low budget.

From past experiences we knew that visual aids were an effective tool in foreign language teaching, but at that time we had little more available to us than a handful of tattered, outdated wall charts. We needed visuals that were:

1. Adaptable to teaching many structures and functions at different levels.

2. Appropriate for use with either a large group or with groups of three to six.

3. Easy to store and file.

4. Inexpensive.

We soon found that such a product was not available, and that if we were ever going to have visual aids that would fit our needs, we would have to make them ourselves.

We were able to make enough visual aids over the course of a few inspired weekends to add variety, action and good humor to our teaching methods. Many of our ideas came from children's stories and games, T.V. game shows, professional journals and fellow teachers. We adapted these ideas to the teaching method we were using.

We tried to keep in mind that a visual should be workable for different types of lessons —introduction, practice, review— and that each should be usable at different levels —beginner, intermediate and advanced. Our ideal visual was one that could be adapted to every level and lesson we taught. Our other consideration was that the student should be able to go from practice with the visual to real communication. In other words, we felt that a visual should not be an end in itself, but rather the starting point for a better understanding and use of the target language.

Because of our success using the materials, we began giving seminars on how to make and use visual aids. After giving the seminar many times and listening to the favorable response, we decided to put our ideas in the form of this book.

We wish to thank the many people who gave us suggestions, criticism and encouragement throughout this project. We hope that they will recognize their contribution and that each person who uses this book will find it a practical addition to his/her teaching methods.

Good luck.

INTRODUCTION

The use of visual aids is a vital part of an effective language program. Much of our learning outside the classroom is through visual media (T.V., movies, billboards, magazines, etc.); therefore we, as teachers, should capitalize on our students' ability to learn with the help of visual aids. A simple drawing or magazine picture can often represent an idea or can be used to show the use of a grammar structure more quickly and effectively than a verbal explanation. A well-chosen visual clue demonstrates how and why the student should use a particular type of language, and because the clue is visual, it stays in the student's mind longer than a lengthy explanation.

ANYONE CAN

DON'T PANIC!!

This book is especially for the person who says: "I can't draw a straight line." Artistic ability or the lack of it should be the least of your worries in making a visual aid. You will notice very few "straight lines" in our examples.

With magazine pictures or simple drawings, even the most "unartistic" can make visual aids that are effective. Children's drawings are a good source of ideas and patterns because of their simplicity and directness.

Two ideas to keep in mind when making a visual aid for your classroom:

(1) Make it as direct and clear as possible.

(2) Keep it simple.

INTRODUCTION

A cluttered color poster may be a work of art, but will confuse the student or be unnecessarily complicated for the teacher to make. Usually, a simple stick figure will convey the idea to the student and will not require a great amount of preparation time and effort on the teacher's part. Also, a simple drawing is much easier to replace than a complicated one. The main objective in making a visual aid is to use a minimum of materials and time to find a way to present a concept clearly and simply.

Finally, when making a visual, think about how many different ways you can use it. Most of the visual aids presented here can be used for more than one activity, or to present more than one structure. Several ideas for using each visual are given and we hope these will help you think of even more ideas that are adaptable to your particular class level and age group.

BRIGHT IDEA

Storage, handling and the time involved in making a visual should be considered before starting. One good idea developed into a useful visual aid is better than three or four "so-so" ideas that lead to less effective visuals. When pondering your idea consider the size, level and ability of your class; plan a visual that will create the maximum participation and involvement of the group. Also try to be open to the possibility of changing and adapting the visual to suit your needs. Visuals do take time and effort to make, so be sure your ideas are clearly thought out and worthy of the time and energy spent on them.

GOOD PLANNING

Good planning is essential to making effective visual aids.
- It is important to place drawings or pictures in several positions before gluing. Decide what looks best to you.
- Do all lettering in pencil first, so you are sure the letters will fit before using an ink marker or paint.
- Write big. Remember, the visual impact of your idea must be clear to the last person in the back row. Drawings, pictures and lettering should be big enough to use with your entire class but small enough to be handled by groups of three to six students.

INTRODUCTION

- All pictures, drawings, and lettering should have strong contrast so they can be seen easily. Black on white produces the best contrast. Use colors for emphasis or contrast when necessary.

GENERAL INFORMATION

Here are some ideas that are important for making the most of visual aids.

1. **POSTER PAPER**
   This is any type of paper that is strong enough to withstand the wear and tear of classroom use.

2. **TAPE**
   Taping all the edges with plastic tape helps protect the visual and prolong its life. Put a strip of plastic tape on all the edges of both sides of the visual. This adds strength as well as color and serves as a frame for the visual.

3. DOUBLE-SIZE POSTER

Follow the instructions for taping as described in No. 2 for two pieces of poster paper. After all edges are taped, place the two pieces of paper side by side, lining up the edges. Carefully tape the joint on both sides. This gives you a large poster that can be easily folded, and therefore more easily stored or carried.

4. WIRE

Stretch a strong wire along the top of the blackboard from one corner to the other. Attach the wire to the wall or the blackboard with nails or screws. Place clothespins along the length of the wire. Now you can pin your visuals on the wire for your class to see whenever necessary.

5. CORNER FRAMES

Corner frames are gummed paper corners that are used for mounting photographs in a picture album. We use them in our visuals when we have a set of cards or pictures that need to be changed in order to provide more practice with the visual.

6. MATERIALS NEEDED

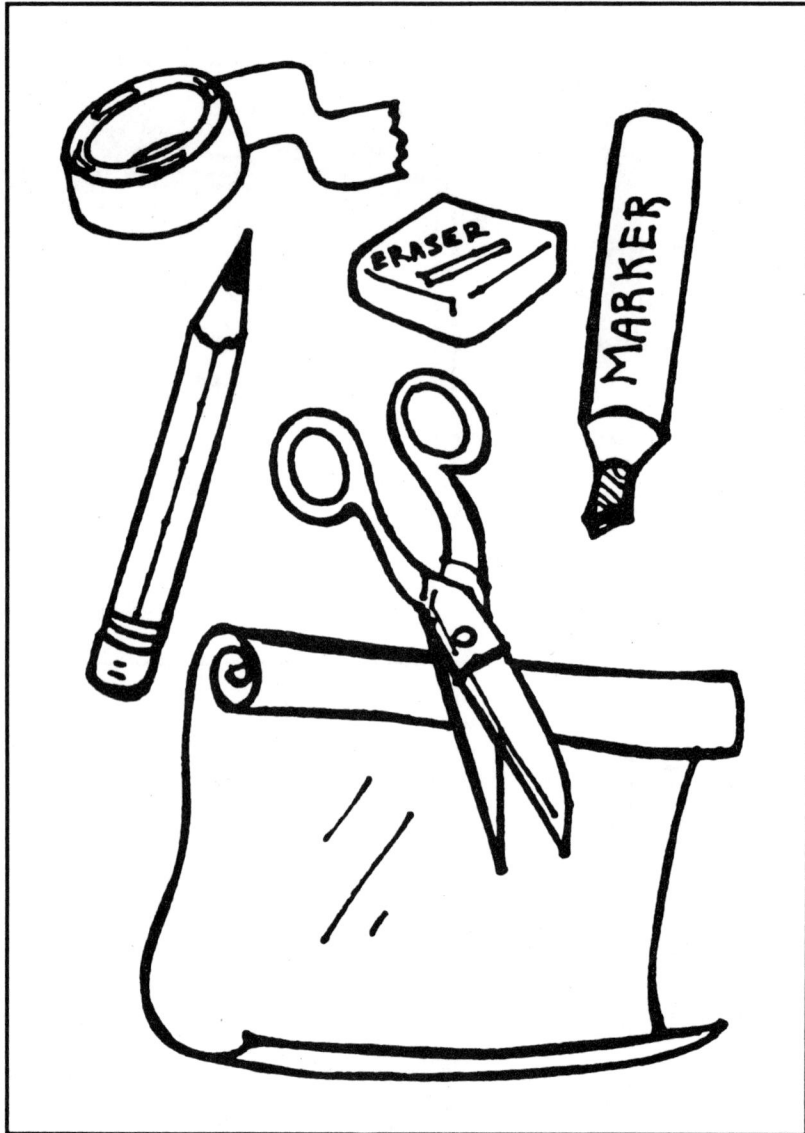

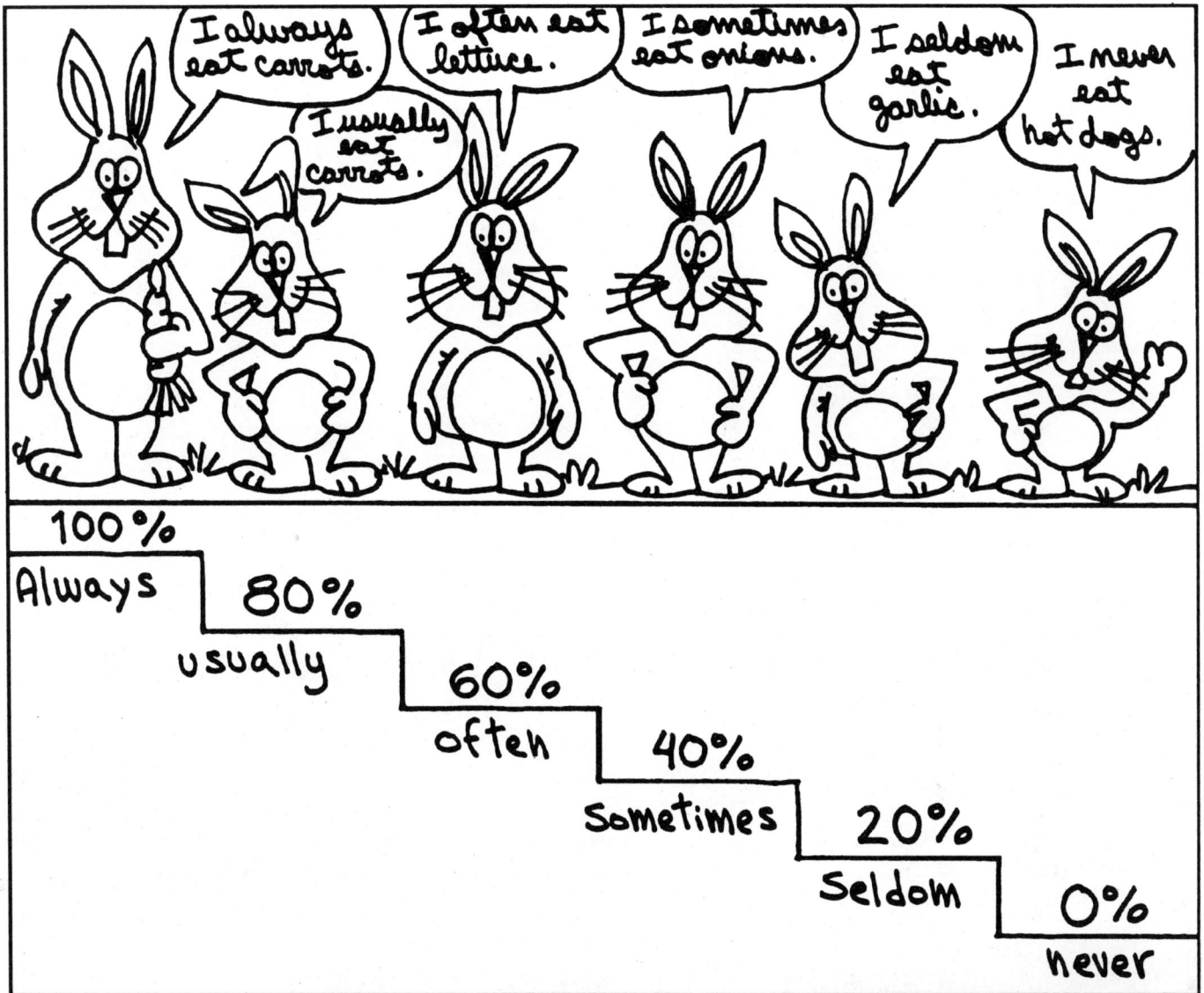

Explanation

This is a useful visual for basic courses. It demonstrates the concept of frequency words with percentages and drawings. The visual should be used as a starting point. Students should eventually communicate personal information.

HOW TO MAKE IT

1. Collect six magazine pictures of people with a big smile showing their teeth, or make simple drawings of smiling faces.

2. Cut out the six pictures and glue them to the poster paper. Under the first one, put the word ALWAYS; under the second one, write USUALLY; under the third one, write OFTEN; under the fourth one, put SOMETIMES; under the fifth one, put SELDOM; and, under the sixth one, write NEVER.

3. Leave the first picture as it is, but in the succeeding five pictures black out some of the teeth. Black out a couple of teeth for USUALLY, a few more for OFTEN, and so on. NEVER will have all the teeth blacked out.

4. At the top of the poster write these questions:
   a. "How often do they go to the dentist?"
   b. "How often do they brush their teeth?"
   c. "How often do they eat candy?"

NOTE: Question c will show you if your students understand the frequency words because they will have to change the words they use with the characters.

How often do they go to the dentist?
How often do they brush their teeth?
How often do they eat candy?

always usually often sometimes seldom never

5. On the other side of the poster write the frequency words in the same order that you used in step 4.

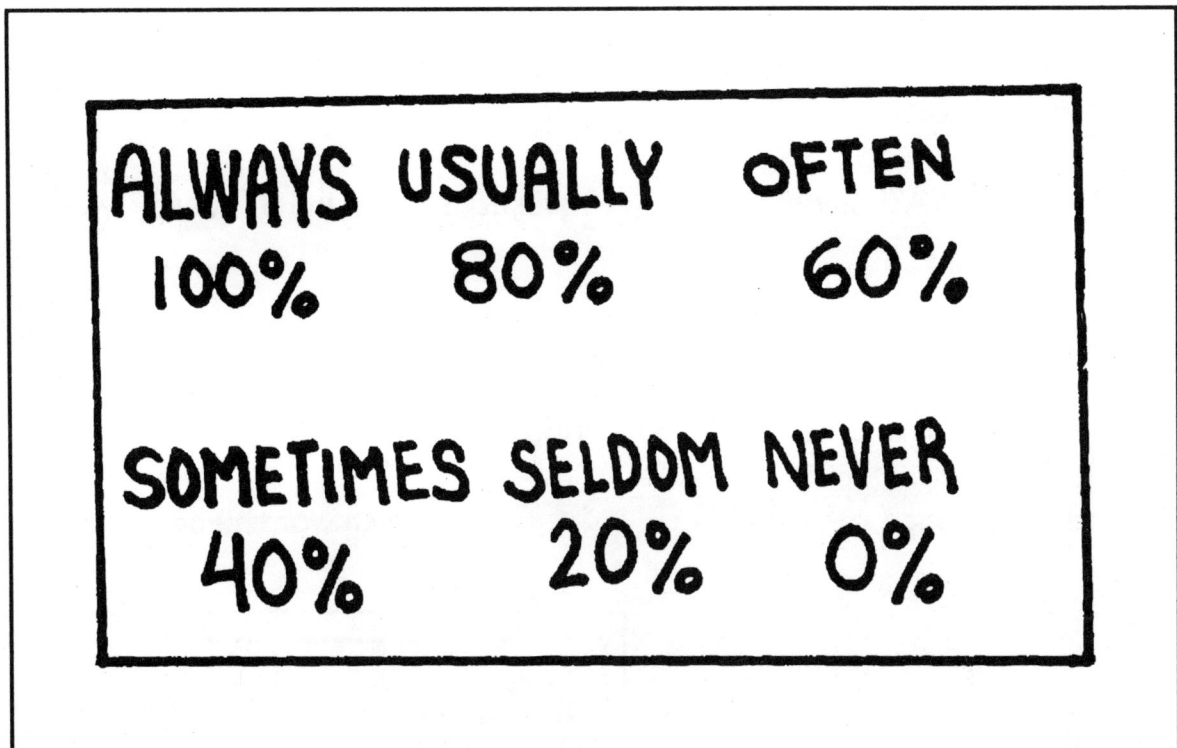

ALWAYS   USUALLY   OFTEN
100%   80%   60%

SOMETIMES SELDOM NEVER
40%   20%   0%

6. Under ALWAYS write 100% of the time.
Under USUALLY write 80% of the time.
Under OFTEN write 60% of the time.
Under SOMETIMES write 40% of the time.
Under SELDOM write 20% of the time.
Under NEVER write 0% of the time.

NOTE: This visual could easily be drawn on the blackboard.

FREQUENCY WORDS

Teacher-led activity

1. Show the percentage side of the poster. Go over the idea of frequency words, using the poster as a guide.

2. Ask students to answer questions about the frequency words.

Examples:

"Which word means Monday, Wednesday, Friday?"

"Which word means once a week?"   "Which word means once a month?"

3. When you are sure the students understand the meaning of each frequency word, draw this diagram on the blackboard.

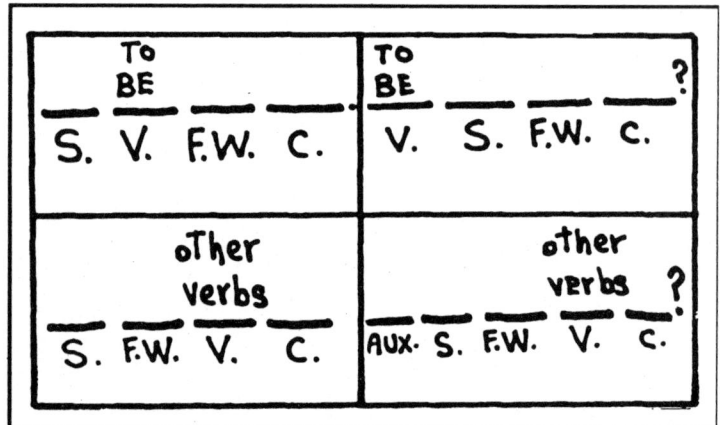

TO BE _ _ _ _ .	TO BE _ _ _ _ ?
S. V. F.W. C.	V. S. F.W. C.
other verbs _ _ _ _ .	other verbs _ _ _ _ ?
S. F.W. V. C.	AUX. S. F.W. V. C.

4. Show the side of the poster with the faces. Ask the students to answer the questions:
   a. "How often do they go to the dentist?"
   b. "How often do they brush their teeth?"
   c. "How often do they eat candy?"

Individual work

Ask the students to write about their family and/or friends using frequency words.

Example:
"My friend Alice never goes to class on Friday."
"My brother always washes his car on Saturday."

Group work

Divide the class into groups of three to six, and have them ask each other logical questions about their family and friends using frequency words.

Additional exercise

Have students talk in pairs.

Example:
Student 1: "Do you sometimes _____?"   Student 2: "No, I don't, but I often_____

                                                        Do you too?"

Student 1: "I never_____."   Student 2: "Why not?"
Student 1: "_____."
This will lead students into a short discussion.

Follow-up exercise

Kathy and John always get to work on time. They usually eat lunch downtown. They usually eat in a French restaurant. They often go out of town on the weekend. They always go to Acapulco in the fall. They seldom go to the movies.

Write this paragraph on the blackboard.

FREQUENCY WORDS

Ask the students to write questions based on the paragraph using frequency words. Ask them to ask for additional information using the following words. Write this list on the blackboard.

1.	Chinese restaurant	6.	after work
2.	sleepy in class	7.	the movies
3.	work late	8.	early
4.	Sunday morning	9.	homework
5.	in the summer	10.	on Fridays

Examples:

Information: They usually eat in a French restaurant.
Student's question: "Do they sometimes eat in a Chinese restaurant?"

Information: They always go to Acapulco in the fall.
Student's question: "What do they usually do in the summer?"

Information: Kathy never gets to work late.
Student's question: "Does she usually work on Saturday?"

OPPOSITES

DOWN
UP
TALL
SHORT
HAPPY
SAD
OPPOSITES
OPPOSITES
LATER
NOW
HOT
COLD
YES
NO
OVER
ABOVE
BLACK
WHITE

Explanation

Unlike most of the visuals in this guide, this visual has basically one purpose and use: learning opposites. It could be used to introduce the lesson, to test the results, or as a game to practice the use of words with opposite meanings.

HOW
TO
MAKE IT

1. Cut out large geometric shapes.

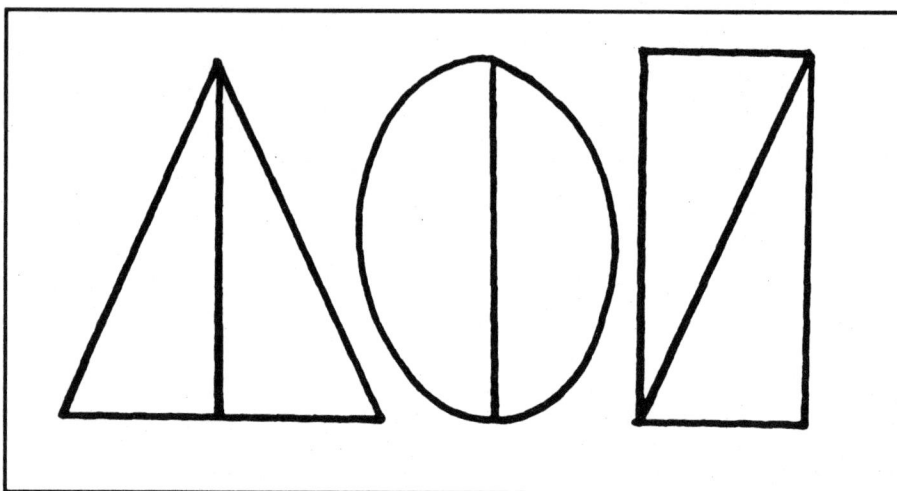

2. Draw a line to divide
each shape in half.

3. Write two words with opposite meanings on either side of the line on each shape.

HOT COLD / UP DOWN / OVER UNDER

4. Glue the shapes on a large piece of poster paper.

5. Write an example that is an obvious error such as:

married – happy   cold – icy

OPPOSITES

6. The words you use will depend on the level you are teaching, and categories can be mixed or matched depending on the ability of your group. Possible categories:

a. **Verbs**

    stand up - sit down
    talk - be silent
    laugh - cry
    shout - whisper

b. **Adjectives**

    hot - cold
    tall - short
    angry - happy
    easy - difficult

c. **Nouns**

    ice - fire
    earth - sky
    peace - war
    desert - forest

d. **Prepositions**

    up - down
    into - out of
    in front of - behind
    for - against

e. **Adverbs**

    slowly - quickly
    carefully - recklessly
    tightly - loosely
    softly - loudly

Teacher-led activity

1. Show the visual to the whole class and ask them to read and comment on it.

2. When they notice the "error," talk about what the opposite of each word should be. Use these words as a take-off point for group or individual work.

3. Using HAPPY/MARRIED for example, ask the students the opposite of **happy**. Ask them to think of other emotions and feelings. They should come up with words like **joyful**, **melancholy**, **sleepy**, **hungry**, **depressed**, **angry**, etc. Have them tell or write the opposite word. Repeat the process with **married**.

4. Using the word **married** as the example, ask the students the opposite. They will say **single**. Ask them what other words they think of when they hear the word **single**. They will say **young**, **playboy**, **student**, and so on. Write these words on the blackboard.

Do the same process with **married**. They will think of **parent**, **family**, **children**, **bride**, **groom**, **church**, **home**, etc. Also write these words on the blackboard.

Ask the students to find words with opposite meanings for the words on the blackboard where possible.

Hint: Have students use a dictionary because they will know many words in the native language but not in the target language.

OPPOSITES

Individual work

Give each student a list of words and a dictionary. Ask the students to write sentences using the words and their opposite meanings.

Group work

a. Large group game:
    Divide the class into two or three groups. Have the first group say any word and use it in a sentence. Then have the second group say the opposite and use it in a sentence.

b. Small group game:
    Give the group a list of words and have them decide on words with opposite meanings either orally or in writing.

Additional exercise

Give the small groups ten to fifteen minutes to discuss the words they've studied. This usually turns into "free conversation" using the words studied. Make yourself available to help students to use a dictionary and to ask questions related to the topics they are discussing. This "free" time allows students to clear up doubts they may have about different words and their meanings.

3 SCRAMBLED WORDS

step 1.

Teacher	doctor	Taxi driver
Businessman	dancer	bartender
singer	cowboy	flight Attendant

WRITE THE CORRECT WORD ON THE POSTER PAPER

step 2.

TAPE CARDS OVER THE WORDS

tape here

taxi driver

bartender

flight Attendant

step 3.

WRITE THE SCRAMBLED WORD ON THE COVER CARD

ercheat	roocdt	viia redrat
namssenisu	rechad	raterbend
gerins	yoobwc	tietta dlaghfntn

Explanation

This is an easy-to-make, simple-to-use visual that is an excellent way to review and practice vocabulary and spelling. Students are presented scrambled words that they must recognize and correctly spell. The words are grouped into sets according to

SCRAMBLED WORDS

categories such as:

```
adjectives
occupations
prepositions
parts of the body
things in the classroom
clothing
animals
fruit
colors
proper names
capitals of the world
vegetables
```

The teacher can lead discussions about the word categories and why some words fit the category and why others do not.

One advantage of this visual is that students cannot translate; therefore, they must think and spell in English. Thinking in the native language will not help them; in fact, it will distract them.

Example:

Correct English word: S I N G E R.
Scrambled English word: G E R I N S.

HOW TO MAKE IT

1. Tape two pieces of poster paper together.

2. Divide each piece of poster paper into at least five, but not more than twelve, equal sections. This allows space for ten to twenty-four words, one word in each section.

3. Select words from a particular category. We have used professions in the example. You could choose any group of words that have already been presented to your students.

4. Write these words in the sections on your poster paper, one word for each section. (See drawing.)

5. Cut out cards that will cover the sections on the poster paper, covering the word underneath.

SCRAMBLED WORDS

6. Place the cut-out cards over the words and tape them at the top, half the tape on the card and half of the tape on the poster paper. This will enable you to flip the cards up.

7. Write the same words that appear on the visual in a scrambled form on the cards.

Examples:

dancer – nardec

doctor – rocotd

nurse – serun

dentist – tentdsi

HOW TO USE IT

Teacher-led activity

1. Divide your class into two teams.

2. Explain that these are scrambled words from a specific category and the object is to identify and spell the words correctly.

3. A student from **Team A** selects a scrambled word. (You can number the words or have the students give directions, such as "the word at the bottom of the third column.")

4. A student from **Team B** must say what the correct form of the scrambled word is, spell it correctly, and then use it in a sentence. If the sentence is correct, his/her team gets a point. Lift up the card with the scrambled word on it and let the class see the correctly spelled word underneath. If the student is correct, then his/her team gets a second point. If he/she is wrong, then the team gets only one point.

5. Reverse the process. **Team B** selects the word and **Team A** attempts to unscramble it and use it in a sentence.

Individual work

1. Teacher explains the visual.

2. Each student is responsible for unscrambling all the words. He/she will write each word in a sentence.

SCRAMBLED WORDS

3. Once he/she has finished with all the words that appear on the visual, he/she can check the answers by looking under the cards at the correct word or the teacher can collect the papers and correct them.

4. Have students add more words that fit in the same category.

5. Discuss why some of the words suggested by the students either belong or do not belong to the particular category.

Group work

1. The teacher explains the visual.

2. Follow the same procedure that is described for individual work above, but have students work together in groups of three to six. Students will unscramble the words, write a sentence for each word, and add as many words as they can to the list.

Explanation

This visual is a game that can be adapted to almost any structure and age level. We have chosen the dragon and the princess as our theme. You could choose almost any two groups, two animals, two people, or any other subject that suggests the "something versus something" situation. (See no. 8 below.)

HOW TO MAKE IT

1. Tape the edges of two large pieces of poster paper.

2. On one poster draw the pursuing character (in our example, the dragon.)

3. On the other draw the heroine or the one being pursued (in our example, a lovely princess.)

4. On both sides of the heroine punch holes. Insert a paper clip that has been bent to form a hook in each hole on both sides of the princess. Tape the clips securely on the back side of the poster, leaving the hooked part sticking through the poster on the front.

5. String yarn, twine, string, or cord across the heroine from hook to hook, giving the appearance that she is bound. The number of lines of cord strung across the princess must correspond to the number of questions that will be asked.

6. Place the dragon at one end of the blackboard and the princess at the other end. Draw waves between the dragon and the princess. Draw the same number of waves as you have lines of cord binding the princess.

10
Lines of
cord

10 waves

7. The idea of the game is that the dragon must cross the ten waves to get on the island where the princess is. The rope crosses the princess ten times; therefore, she has ten ropes to untie before she can escape from the dragon.

8. Possible themes for the game besides a dragon and a princess:

1. radicals and hostages
2. cannibal and missionary
3. good guys and bad guys
4. cops and robbers
5. cat and bird in a cage
6. little fish and shark

HOW TO USE IT

Group work

1. Divide the class into two groups.

2. Have each group decide what they represent, the princess or the dragon.

3. The teacher is the referee and the final decision maker.

4. The game can be played several ways. One possibility is the following:

   a. Have the dragon ask a question. If it is correct, he advances one wave.
   b. Have the princess answer the question. If it is correct, untie one rope.
   c. Continue in this manner until one of the characters wins. The dragon wins if all the waves are erased before all the ropes are untied from the princess. The princess wins if she escapes from her ropes before the dragon gets across the waves to her.
   d. If the game ends in a tie, start again.

Uses

Almost any grammar structure or function can be adapted to this game. Here is a partial list:

1. Passive voice vs. active voice: Have the first character say a logical sentence in the active voice and the second character repeat the information using the passive voice structure.

Example:

Dragon: Dr. Johnson has operated on my uncle six times.

Princess.: My uncle has been operated on six times.

2. **Past tense vs. past perfect:** Have the first character say a sentence in the definite past tense and the second character ask a question or repeat the same information, changing it to the past perfect tense.

Example:

Dragon: The thief left before the police arrived.

Princess: The thief had already left when the police arrived.

3. **Past tense vs. future:** Have one group give information, using either the definite past or the future, and the second group ask for more information in the other tense.

Example:

Dragon: My grandmother went to Acapulco several months ago.

Princess: Is she going to stay in Acapulco a long time?

4. **Present of custom vs. present progressive:**

Example:

Dragon: Do you always have your class at this hour?

Princess: No, I don't. I'm visiting today.

5. Past tense vs. present tense:

Example:

        Dragon: Were you sick yesterday?
        Princess: No, I wasn't, but I have a headache today.

6. Functions: Have the first group ask or give information, introduce someone, or ask for directions.

Example:

        Dragon: Where can I get a good hamburger near here?
        Princess: George's Restaurant has very good hamburgers. It's on this street between Fourth Avenue and Park Place.

5 SOMETHING'S WRONG

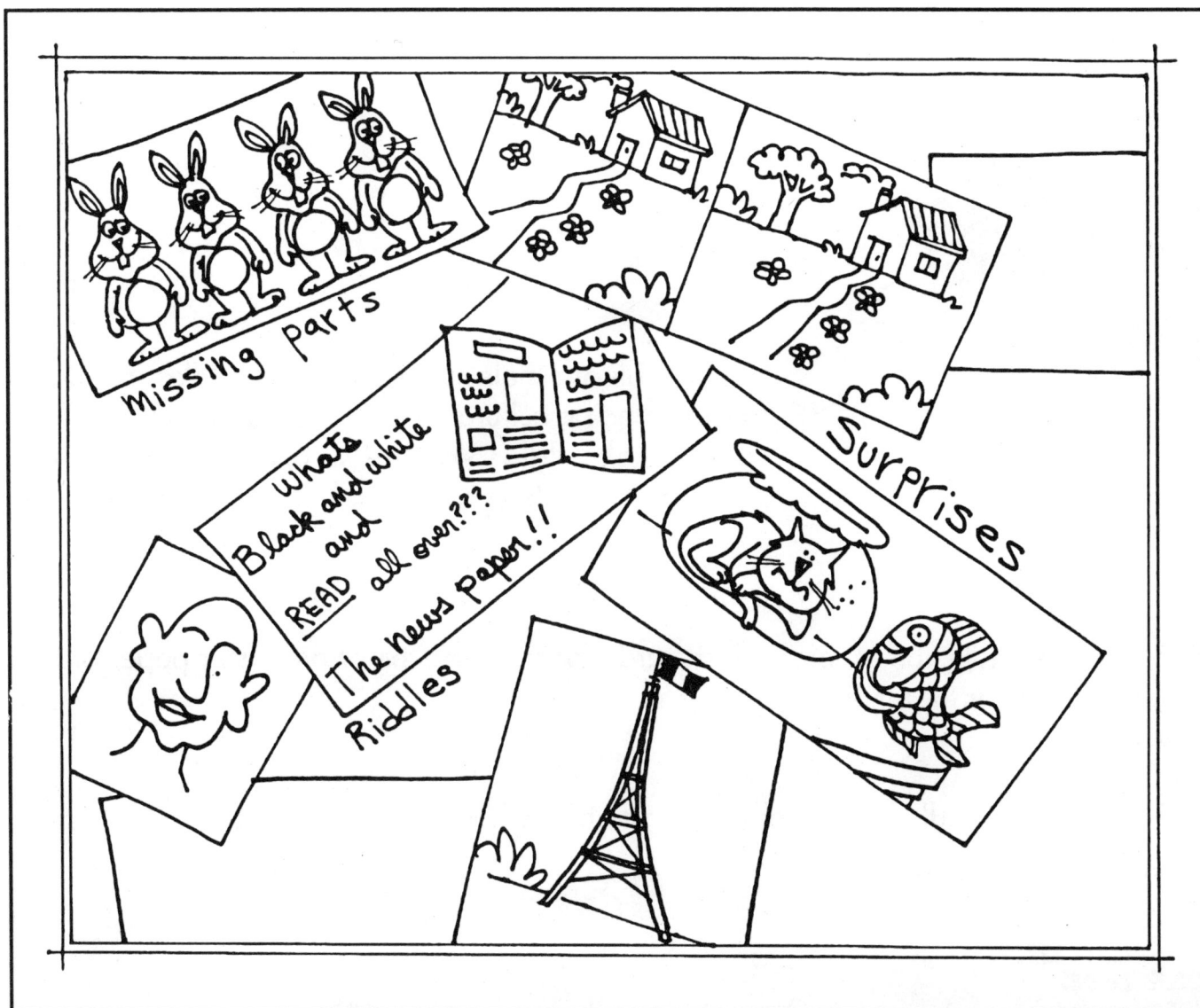

missing parts

What's Black and white and READ all over??? The newspaper!!

Riddles

Surprises

Explanation

This is a group of different visual aids, ideas and objects that we have put under the heading "Something's Wrong!" They can be used when you want your students to solve problems. The objective of problem solving in the English language class is to get the students thinking and speaking in the target language.

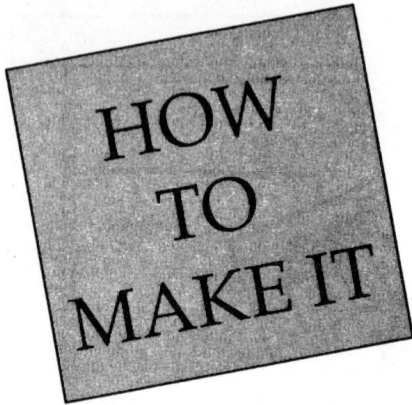
HOW TO MAKE IT

I. RIDDLES

1. Find a book of simple riddles. Choose riddles that don't require specific cultural information to answer. In other words, pick riddles you are sure your students will understand even though it may take a while to figure them out.

2. Write the riddles on separate flash cards for small groups or on poster paper or the blackboard for the whole class.

3. Make several riddle flash cards that can be passed from group to group.

Examples:

– What's found in the middle of America, in North but not in South?
  Answer: The letter R.

– A sign before all railroad tracks in the U.S.A. "Railroad crossing. Look out for the cars."
  Can you spell that without any R's?
  Answer: T H A T

– What's black and white and read all over?
Read this riddle to your class. Later show the class the written form so they understand the riddle.

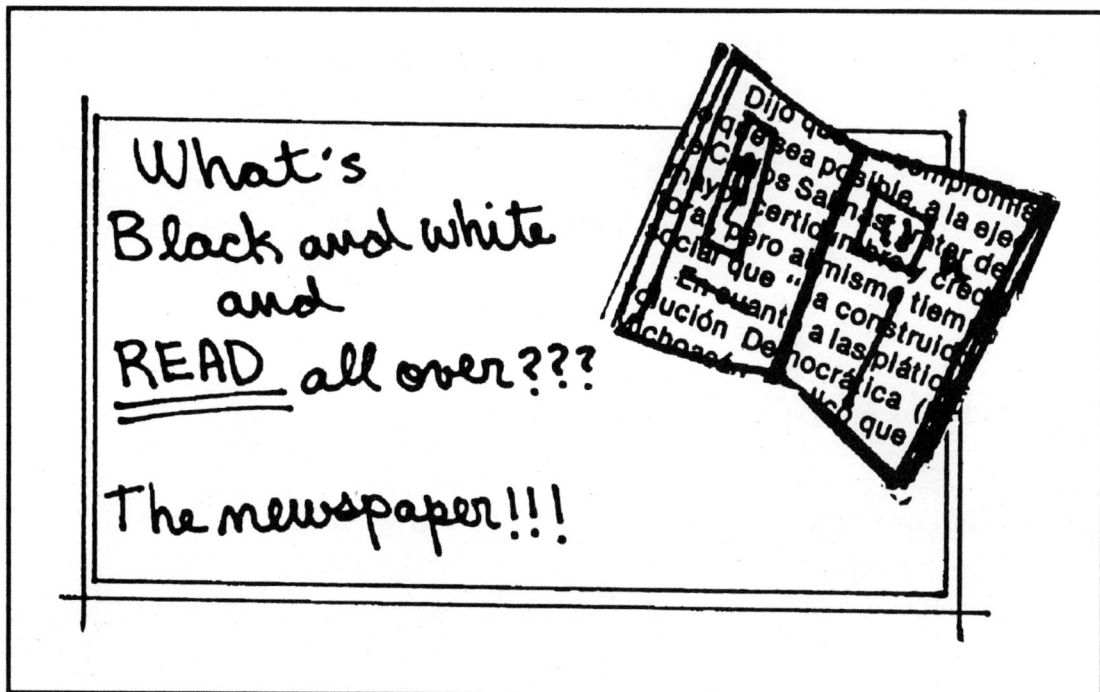

II. SCRAMBLED WORDS

This is a very effective exercise, and we have written a unit about it. (See Chapter Three.)

HOW
TO
MAKE IT

III. MISSING PARTS

This is an exercise that has familiar pictures with parts missing or changed. A picture is shown to the students for one or two seconds. The students then report what is missing or different in the picture. This helps train students to look, think, and speak quickly. It will also help students break the translation habit.

HOW TO MAKE IT #1

1. Copy an object or person several times, being sure that each one is exactly the same.

2. Make a slight change or omission on one of the examples.

HOW TO MAKE IT #2

1. Make several flash cards of familiar characters. Use characters from the students' book if possible.

2. Leave out an important detail of the character (nose, ear, eye, hat, etc.).

HOW TO MAKE IT #3

1. Make two scenes (possible items in the scene: tree, house, flowers).

2. Make one picture complete. Make the second with something missing.

HOW TO USE IT

1. Show the flash card to the class for one or two seconds and have them tell you what is missing or different. Students should see the card very briefly so they will have to pay attention and notice details very quickly.

2. Have the students do the above exercise in small groups with one student as the leader.

HINT: If you have a large class and don't want them to be too noisy, have students write down what they thought was missing. Students can check their answers by looking carefully at each visual.

HOW TO MAKE IT

IV. SURPRISES

This visual uses a picture of a familiar scene that includes something obviously out of place. The students must look at the picture quickly and find the part that does not fit.

HOW TO MAKE IT #1

Draw a familiar scene (rooms in a house, a school, a park, etc.). In this very usual scene put something that is definitely "unusual."

HOW TO MAKE IT #2

Cut out pictures of famous people and glue them to a piece of poster paper. Cut out other objects and parts of pictures. Combine the objects and pieces with the pictures of famous people to form a surprise collage.
Possible pictures:

a. Santa Claus in a bathing suit.
b. Julia Roberts with a mustache or with no teeth.
c. Tarzan with a tuxedo.
d. Elizabeth Taylor bald.

HOW TO MAKE IT #3

Make a collage of famous places, objects, or landmarks, adding absurd details.

Possible pictures:

a. The Statue of Liberty with a lightbulb in place of the torch.
b. The Sphinx with a sun hat or umbrella.
c. Venus de Milo wearing a bikini.

HOW TO USE IT

1. Show the visual to the class for one or two seconds and have them tell you what the surprise is. Students should see the card briefly so they will have to pay attention and notice details quickly.

2. Have the students do the above exercise in small groups with one student as the leader.

HOW TO MAKE IT

V. GRAB BAG

Fill a bag with familiar objects that usually go together. Put one object in the bag that is obviously different from the rest of the group. All objects must be easily identifiable. Possible Grab Bag items:

Bag 1:
    Table knife, fork, spoon, comb.
Bag 2:
    Hairbrush, comb, hair roller, toothbrush.
Bag 3:
    Spool of thread, button, zipper, coffee cup.

Bag 4:
    Hammer, pliers, wrench, seashell.
Bag 5:
    Pencil, notebook, eraser, small flowerpot.

HOW TO USE IT

Have a student put his/her hand in the bag and identify each item by feeling it. The student must decide which items go together and which one is out of place. Several other students can do the same exercise. Finally, the contents of the bag can be emptied so that the students can check their answers.

GRAB BAG #4

Notebook

GRAB BAG #5

Explanation

This flip chart provides a method for practicing those difficult word order structures using the verbs WANT, ASK, TELL, ADVISE, INVITE. The students practice the word order with various subjects, verbs, and complements provided by the flip chart. The last piece of paper in each set has a question mark, so the student must come up with an original sentence using the correct word order.

HOW TO MAKE IT

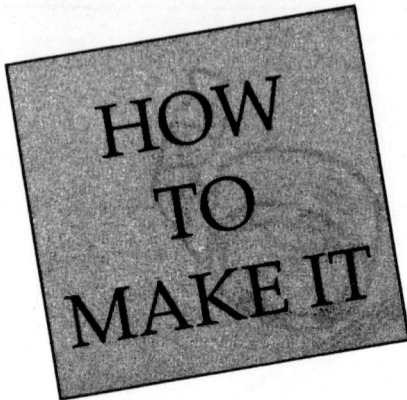

1. Cut the cards that you are going to tape on the poster paper. Cut five cards for each part of the sentence:

   5 - Subject cards
   5 - Verb cards
   5 - Indirect object cards
   5 - Cards to suggest the infinitive of a verb

HINT: Use different lengths or colors of cards for each of the four categories.

2. Draw simple stick pictures of people on the **subject** and **indirect object** cards.

3. Draw simple symbols to suggest the **infinitive of a verb** on one set of cards.

4. Write the **verbs** WANT, ASK, TELL, ADVISE, INVITE on one set of cards.

5. Make a question mark on the last card in each set.

6. Tape the four cards with question marks to the poster paper. Now tape each **subject** card on top of the first card, tape each **verb** card on top of the second card, each **indirect object** on the third, etc.

HINT: Before taping the cards decide on the best arrangement.

HOW TO USE IT

GENERAL INFORMATION FOR ALL STRUCTURES

Explain the pattern: S + V + I O + TO + V to your class. Give them several sample sentences using the verbs WANT, ASK, TELL, ADVISE, INVITE. Have a student read the first sample sentence that is shown on the cards. Then flip one of the cards over, for example the subject, and ask a different student to form a sentence. You can change the subject, indirect object, verb, or complement by flipping the cards over. At the end, all the cards will have question marks and you can elicit original examples from the students.

Depending on the level of your class, you may want to tell the students what verb tense to use.

Teacher-led activity

1. Review the grammar structure for these particular verbs as a class warm-up before using the visual. Explain that the visual shows the correct order of subject, verb, indirect object, and TO plus the infinitive form of a verb. The students must form complete sentences or questions, using the visual clues. Tell the students what verb tense to use. You can give clues to indicate the tense (always, last year, etc.)

2. Have the students read the example on the cards.

S.   V.   I.O.   to + V

Mr. Jones wants John to study English.

John told Paul to bring the
English book to class.

3. Flip one of the cards up so that the
example changes.

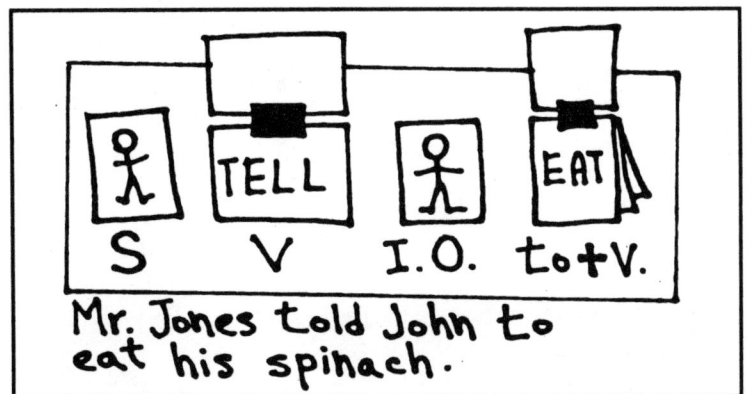

Mr. Jones told John to
eat his spinach.

4. Flip another card up, or two at the
same time, so the student must
make a different sentence.

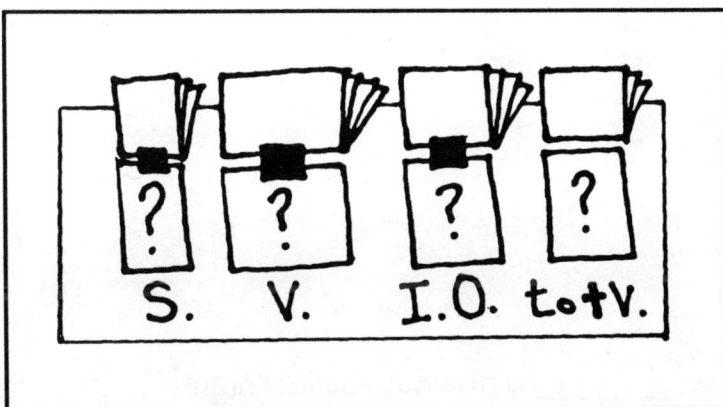

5. Continue with this until all the
cards have question marks.

6. Now elicit original examples from the students. The students can refer to the visual for
help with the word order.

7. Practice the interrogative by placing cards with the auxiliaries DO and DOES in front of the visual and a question mark card at the end.

8. Flip the cards as before so that the students must produce a different example each time.

Group work

Student 1:	
(Gives information)	"Bob wants Sue to buy him an ice cream cone."
Student 2:	
(Asks question)	"Does Sue want to buy one for Bob?"
Student 3:	
(Answers question)	"Yes, she does. She wants one too."

Additional exercise

Student 1:	"Did you ask _____ to go with you last night?"
Student 2:	"Yes, I did." OR "No, I didn't. I _____."
Student 1:	"Why did _____?"
Student 2:	"Because _____."

Explanation

This visual is useful for demonstrating a game that might otherwise be difficult to explain or would have to be explained in the students' native language. This game can be used at any level to get your students talking about themselves. In addition, it makes each student speak clearly in order to be understood and listen carefully to the other students in order to be able to repeat their sentences; therefore, students are practicing both speaking and listening.

HOW TO MAKE IT

1. Tape two large pieces of poster paper together on both sides of the joint.

HINT:

This visual is also effective when drawn on the blackboard.

2. Cut out or draw four or five figures of boys and girls, and paste them to the poster paper. Use pictures of teenagers or adults if your students will identify more closely with them.

3. Choose any structure or function that you want to practice. We have used HE's, SHE's plus the verb TO BE with emotions and feelings in our visual.

4. Write one sentence using the structure or function you have chosen for each character on your poster.

Character 1 will have one sentence in his/her bubble. (The following examples use the present perfect tense.)

The second character will re-state the first character's information ("He's studied English for two years.") and will give some information about himself/herself, using the same structure ("I've lived in Chicago for a year."). Thus the second character will have two sentences in his/her bubble.

The third character must re-state the first and second characters' sentences and give his/her own information and so on. Thus each succeeding bubble must contain an additional sentence.

HOW TO USE IT

Teacher-led activity

Read the sentences on the poster to the class. Then add your own information, following the pattern set up by the poster.

Group work

Students are in groups of five or six. The first student in each group gives his/her example, following the example of the visual, but using his/her own information. The rest of the group is responsible for remembering this example. The next student repeats the first student's example (using he/she) and adds his/her own information. This procedure is repeated around the circle. When everyone has taken a turn, the first student must repeat everyone's examples and give his/her own.

Even at beginning levels, this can be done in English because the students can look at the visual and understand how the activity is to be done. The poster should be visible while the small groups are practicing to remind them of the procedure.

Possible functions:

Introducing yourself –	Example:	"Hello, I'm Alice. I'm from New York."
Expressing emotions –	Example:	"I'm very happy today."
Complaining –	Example:	"I put my money in the machine and didn't get a soft drink."
Giving information –	Example:	"You can get very good hamburgers at Joe's".
Making a suggestion –	Example:	"Let's go to Joe's Restaurant after class."
Expressing desires –	Example:	"I would like to see the movie at the River theater."

LISTEN AND SPEAK

Possible structures:

Past tense —

Example: "Hello, I'm Alice and I was very late today."

Adjective clauses —

Example: "I'm Alice and I came to school with the boy who lives next door to me."

Verbs with two complements —

Example: "I'm Alice and I bought my brother a radio."

Future tense —

Example: "Hello, I'm Alice and I'm going to Acapulco next Saturday."

Possessive pronouns —

Example: "I'm Alice. This book is mine, but this pencil is his."

Explanation

This poster has several uses, but its main use is to practice IN, ON, AT, NEAR and other spatial prepositions. It can also be used for vocabulary building and describing objects because of the variety of things shown in the picture. The poster is a collage of magazine pictures and drawings.

HOW TO MAKE IT

1. Make a collection of big magazine pictures. Collect anything and everything: animals, people, objects, words. The age of your students should help you determine the theme of your collage.

2. Tape the edges of a large piece of poster paper.

3. Arrange the magazine cutouts to make an interesting collage of ideas and colors.

4. Be sure you have arranged cutouts in a manner to include several examples of the prepositions IN, ON, AT and NEAR.

5. When you have decided on the best arrangement of the magazine pictures to form your collage, glue the pieces on the poster paper.

6. If you have small groups of students, several different small posters would be useful.

HOW TO USE IT

Teacher-led activity

Show the poster to the group and ask the students questions or have the students ask questions about the poster.

Where is the _____ ?
Is the _____ on the _____ ?

Individual work

Show the group the poster and explain that it illustrates IN, ON, AT and NEAR. Ask them to write questions using the prepositions. Collect the papers and redistribute them so no one has his/her own set of questions. Ask the students to answer the questions according to what they see on the poster.

Group work

Have students in groups of three or four ask questions based on the poster. One student asks a question and the other members of the group give an answer according to what they see on the poster.

Additional exercise

Prepare a handout with questions that correspond to the poster. Students can answer the questions individually or in small groups.

Example:

Is the rabbit **on** the hat?
Student answer: No, it's **in** the hat.

POSTER

Open-ended exercise

Example:

Is the _____ on the _____ ?
Student answer: _____ .

Is a _____ near a _____ ?
Student answer: _____ .

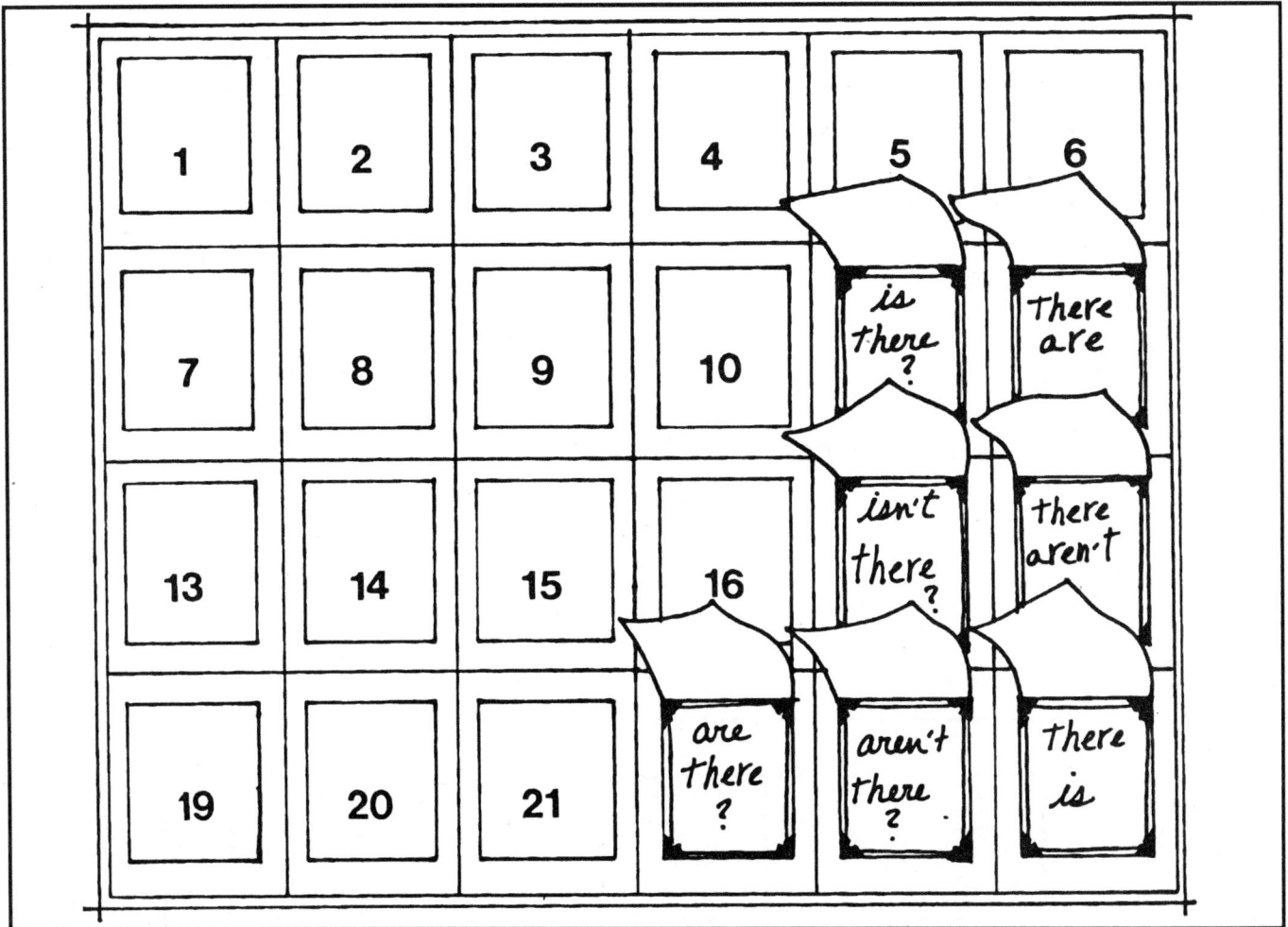

Explanation

This is a visual based on the game "Memory" or "Concentration." It can be used with any structure or function and with any of your classes.

There are twenty-four cards on the visual and each one has a number written on it. Under these cards are cards with a structure or function written on them. There are twelve pairs of structures or functions. The object is to match the pairs and to produce a correct sentence for each structure or function chosen.

1. Tape three pieces of poster paper together.

2. Divide the three pieces of poster paper into twenty-four equal squares, eight squares per sheet.

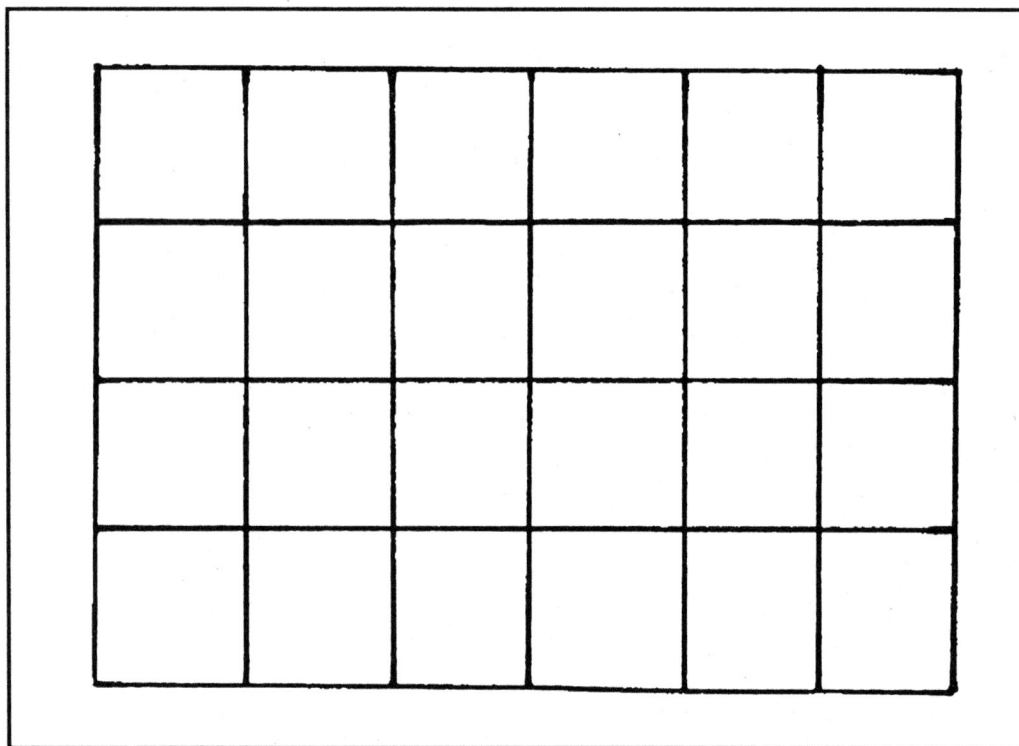

3. In the spaces you have marked off, glue picture corners where you will insert the cards with the structures or functions to be used.

4. Select the structure or functions you want to practice.

5. Cut twenty-four cards that will slip into the picture corners.

6. Write twelve pairs of structures or functions you want to practice on the cards. Each structure or function must be written on two cards.

7. Cut out twenty-four cards that will completely cover the squares containing the cards with the structures or functions under them.

8. Number these cards one to twenty-four.

9. Tape the top edge of a numbered card over each of the squares containing a card with a structure or function. The tape will act as a hinge so you can raise and lower the numbered cards to reveal what is under them.

1. Divide the class into two teams.

2. Explain the rules and objective of the game.

3. Student 1 on **Team A** chooses one of the numbered cards.

4. The teacher flips up the numbered card that has been chosen and reveals a structure or function.

5. Student 1 must produce a sentence using the structure or function he/she has chosen.

Examples:

> Is there a horse in the barn?
> Is there a map in the car?

6. The teacher, as referee, decides if the student's answer is right or wrong. If the answer is right, Student 2 from **Team A** chooses a numbered card; if the answer is wrong, play moves to **Team B**.

7. If Student 1 of **Team A** gives a correct answer, Student 2 from **Team A** chooses a number, trying to choose the other card with the same structure or function as the one just chosen by Student 1 of his/her team.

8. Teacher flips up the numbered card that Student 2 has chosen and reveals a structure or function. If the structure or function is the same as the one chosen by Student 1, Student 2 continues; if the card does not match the card chosen by Student 1, play moves to **Team B**.

9. If Student 2 of **Team A** has chosen the card that matches the card chosen by Student 1, he/she gives an example of that structure or function in a sentence.

10. If the teacher judges the sentence to be correct, **Team A** receives a point.

11. If Student 2 either produces an incorrect response, or wins a point, **Team B** then takes its turn to try to match a pair, produce correct sentences, and win a point.

Possible structures: there is/there are interrogative word questions if clauses

Possible functions: greetings and leave takings asking for information giving information

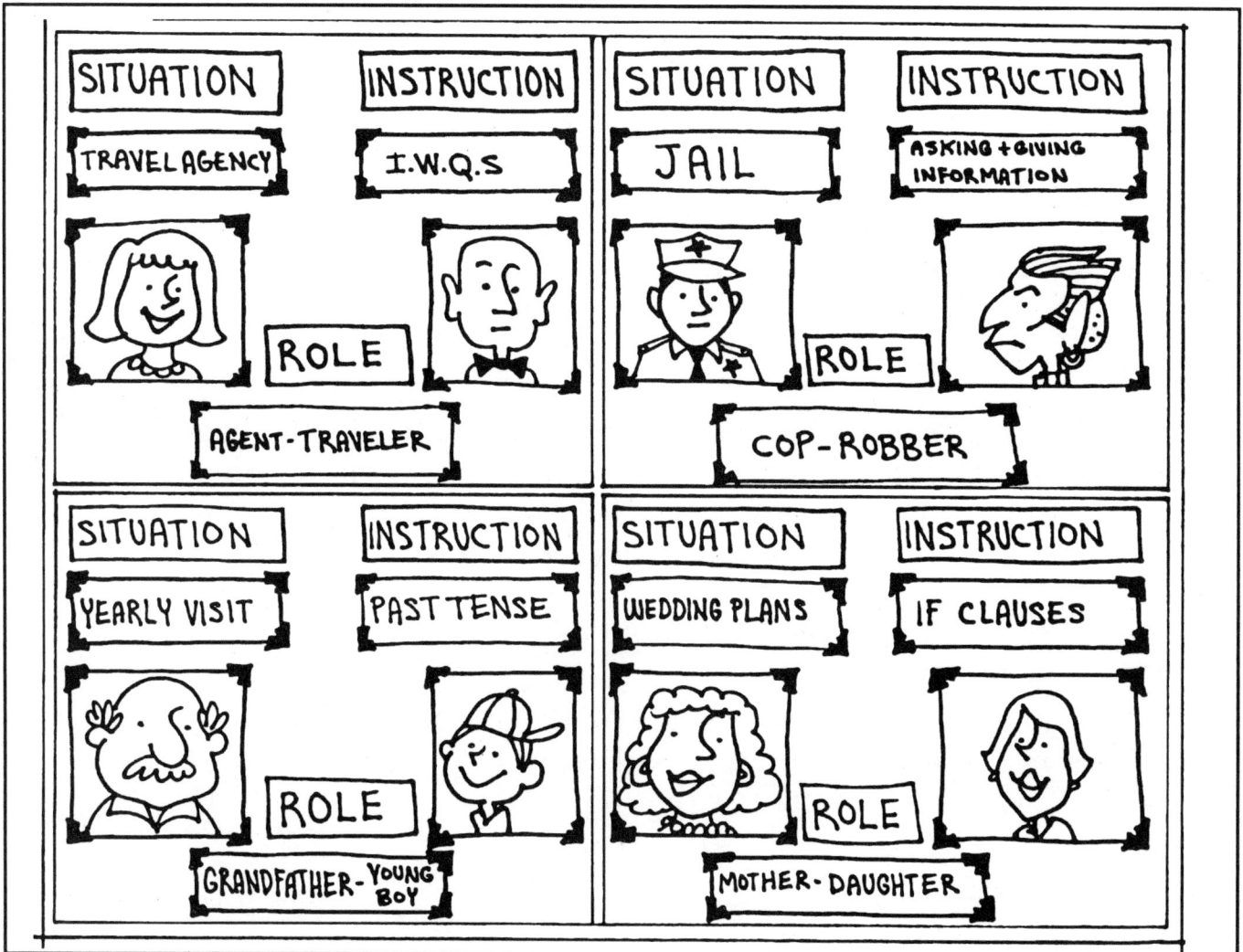

| SITUATION | INSTRUCTION | SITUATION | INSTRUCTION |
| TRAVEL AGENCY | I.W.Q.S | JAIL | ASKING + GIVING INFORMATION |

ROLE
AGENT-TRAVELER

ROLE
COP-ROBBER

| SITUATION | INSTRUCTION | SITUATION | INSTRUCTION |
| YEARLY VISIT | PAST TENSE | WEDDING PLANS | IF CLAUSES |

ROLE
GRANDFATHER-YOUNG BOY

ROLE
MOTHER-DAUGHTER

Explanation

Teachers using functionally based materials will find this visual extremely useful because it provides situations in which students can practice language functions. Teachers using structurally based materials can use this visual for creative activities such as dialogue writing and guided conversation.

The visual shows two characters and has cards indicating (1) the function or structure to be practiced, (2) the situation and (3) the role of the characters.

HOW TO MAKE IT

1. Tape two pieces of poster paper together.

2. In the upper right corner of the poster, write INSTRUCTION. In the upper left corner, write SITUATION. In the center of the poster, approximately one quarter of the distance from the bottom, write ROLE. Under each title, glue four corner frames so that you can easily change the cards in each category.

3. INSTRUCTION CARDS
Cut out cards that will fit under the title INSTRUCTION. Write a structure or function you want your students to practice on each card.

Examples:

STRUCTURE
Simple past tense
If clauses
Present perfect tense
Passive voice
Result clauses

FUNCTION
Inviting
Asking for information
Complaining
Apologizing
Giving directions

4. SITUATION CARDS
Cut out a second set of cards that will fit under the title SITUATION. Write the name of a place or situation on each card, or draw or choose a picture that will suggest a situation.

Examples:

> jail
> party
> classroom
> supermarket
> travel agency
> hotel

5. ROLE CARDS
Cut out a third set of cards that will fit under the title ROLE. Write the roles for two characters on each card.

Examples:

> teacher – student
> parent – teacher
> boyfriend – girlfriend
> doctor – patient
> police officer – thief
> husband – wife

6. These three sets of cards provide many combinations.

FACES

Examples:

```
┌─────────────────────────────┐
│          GRAMMAR            │
│                             │
│ INSTRUCTION – if clauses    │
│ SITUATION – supermarket     │
│ ROLE – husband - wife       │
│                             │
└─────────────────────────────┘
```

```
┌─────────────────────────────┐
│          FUNCTION           │
│                             │
│ INSTRUCTION – asking for and│
│              giving information│
│ SITUATION – jail            │
│ ROLE – police officer – thief│
│                             │
└─────────────────────────────┘
```

7. CHARACTER CARDS

Cut out eight cards to fit in the corner frames under the SITUATION and INSTRUCTION cards. Draw stick figures or find magazine pictures so that you will have the following characters on the eight cards:

```
┌─────────────────────┐
│  1.   one woman     │
│  2.   one woman     │
│  3.   one man       │
│  4.   one man       │
│  5.   one boy       │
│  6.   one boy       │
│  7.   one girl      │
│  8.   one girl      │
└─────────────────────┘
```

This covers all the possibilities of two people conversing (two women, a boy and a man, two girls, etc.).

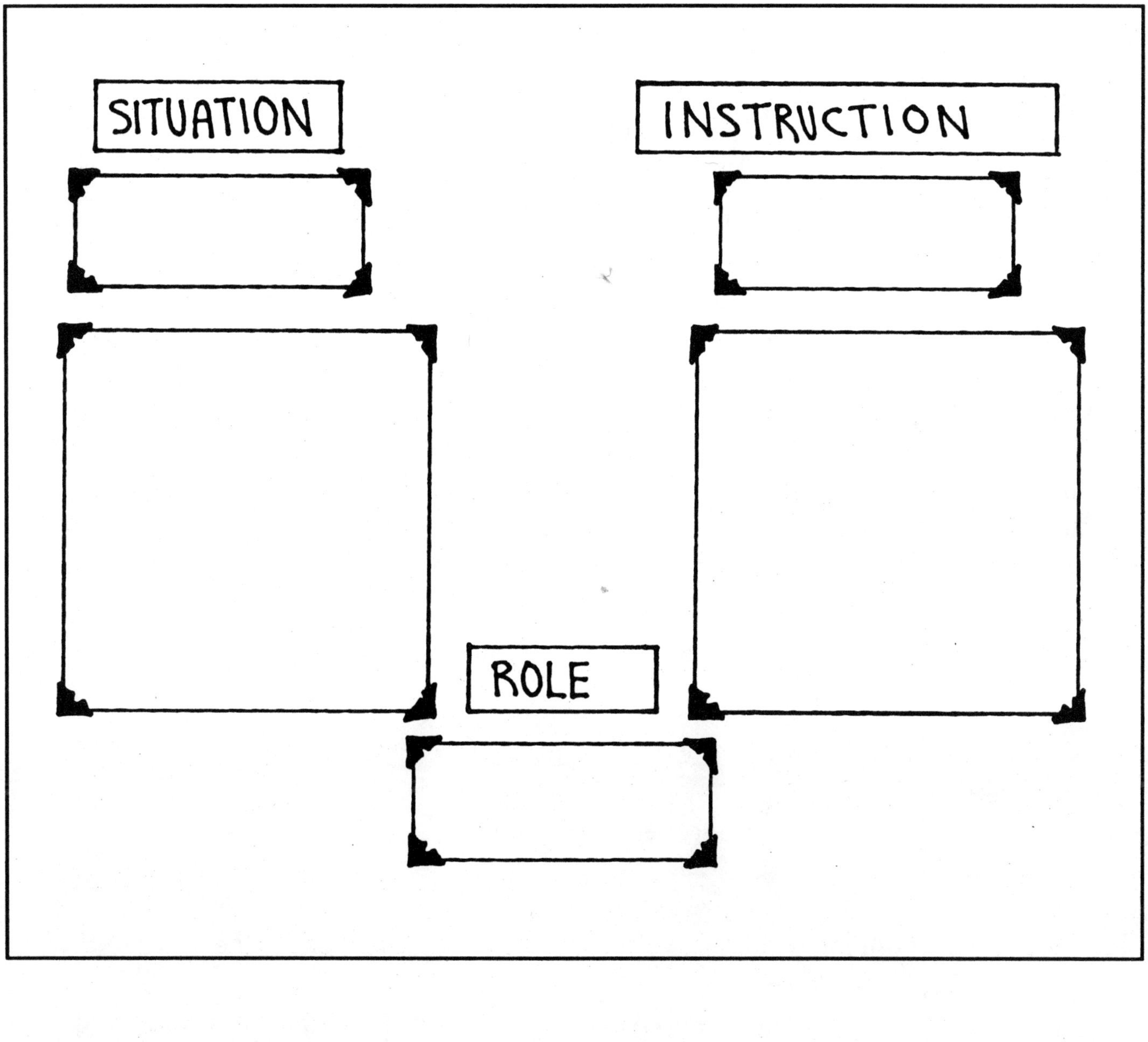

SITUATION

INSTRUCTION

ROLE

HOW TO USE IT

1. Explain the parts of the visual to the students.

2. Explain to the students that they are going to role-play.

Example:
One person is going to take a trip. He goes to a travel agency to arrange his trip and to purchase his ticket. In order to do this, the agent and the traveler must get a lot of information from each other.

3. Put two character cards on the visual, one to represent the agent and one to represent the traveler. (These roles can be changed [male - male, male - female, female - female] to fit the needs of your class.)

4. Place a card under ROLE.

Example:

travel agent – traveler

5. Place a card with the function or structure to be practiced under the word INSTRUC-TION.
For a functionally based course: asking for information, giving information, making suggestions, etc.
For a structurally based class: question words (who, what, when, how often), there is/there are, or another grammar structure.

6. Place a card in the SITUATION position.

Example:

Nancy's
TRAVEL AGENCY

7. Ask a student to act out the situation with you for the whole class.

8. Ask for two volunteers to play the indicated roles for the class.

Student 1: (agent) "Where do you want to go?"
Student 2: (traveler) "I'd like to go to Cancun next Friday."
Student 1: (agent) "When do you want to come back?"
Student 2: (traveler) "Tuesday morning."

9. After the example, ask the class to work in pairs and say or write a dialogue between the two characters on the ROLE cards, each student assuming one of the roles.

10. Remind the students to consider the relationship of the roles to each other (authority, subjective, equal, etc.), and the formality of the situation (formal – informal). This may affect the language they choose for the dialogue.

11. After they have finished the dialogue, ask pairs to present the dialogue to the entire class.

12. Point out that although each pair is playing the same two roles and following the same instructions, the language each pair chooses can be different but correct.

13. Change the instructions leaving the same two roles, or change roles and have the same instructions. Later change both the instructions and roles. Your possibilities are limited only by the number of instructions, roles and situations that you create.

NOTE:

Do not restrict advanced students to one particular structure or function. Give them the situation and the roles and let them use the language that best suits their roles and the situation.

Explanation

This is a multipurpose three-panel poster with pictures that tell a simple story. It can be used with a variety of structures at almost any level. The visual should be big and clearly drawn so the story line is easy to follow.

HOW TO MAKE IT

1. Think of a basic theme and develop a story line.

Examples:

a. Boy meets girl at college.
Couple completes studies.
Couple marries.
Couple lives happily for a while.
Couple has too many children.
Not enough money for fun.
Wife shoots husband.

b. Student begins to study English at your school.
Student gets good grades.
Student graduates.
Student becomes English teacher.
Student becomes rich and buys a big house.

2. Other possible themes:

a. A picnic

b. A vacation

c. Bathing the dog

d. Going to the dentist

3. After you have thought out the story, draw the most important parts. Be sure to follow a logical sequence going from left to right or from top to bottom. Use words only when necessary.

Teacher-led activity

1. Lead the class through the story. Ask questions and acknowledge students' comments.

Example:

"What is he doing in this picture?"   "Do you think he's enjoying himself?"
                 "Why do you think he's happy/unhappy?"

2. Ask students to tell the story. A different student can tell what is going on in each picture.

Individual work

Students write a story based on the visual.

Group work

The class is divided into small groups. Each group tells the story and then continues it logically. Each group can discuss its continuation of the story and then write it. The groups can tell their stories to the whole class.

Suggestions for verb practice:

1. **Simple present tense –** Have students describe the characters in the story.

Example:

Mary has brown eyes.
Her hair is curly.
Bob is tall and thin.
He plays soccer.

For the simple present tense the students can tell the story picture by picture, describing each scene.

2. **Present progressive tense** — Ask the students to describe the actions of the characters.

3. **Future tense** — Go through the story. Leave the visual open so everyone can see the entire story. Begin with the first picture. Ask your students to identify the characters and tell what they are doing in the first picture. When everyone understands the situation in the first picture, ask the class to use the future tense tell what the characters are going to do in the succeeding pictures.

Example:

Student: "John is studying at the university."

Teacher: "What is he going to do when he finishes college?"

Student: "He's going to work at I.B.M. He's going to be the Sales Manager in Mexico City."

4. **Past tense** – Use the same idea as with the future tense, but start at the last picture instead of the first picture. Ask the students to describe the scene in the last picture. Using this as a starting point, ask them to tell what happened in the past. The students recreate the story using the past tense.

5. **Conditional sentences**

Example:

The (character)
could
would
should
might
have

done _____ if _____ .

6. **Passive voice** – Ask the students to tell the story using the passive voice as often as possible.

12

GLOVE PUPPETS

Explanation

One of the most popular forms of entertainment is puppets. Using puppets has also proven to be a very valuable tool in the language classroom. This particular visual has the quality we would like to have in every visual: versatility. Puppets can be used effectively at any

GLOVE PUPPETS

level, with any structure and with any teaching method; therefore, they are ideal for a busy teacher teaching different levels. With careful planning you can use a puppet in every class for one day.

Puppets have also proven to be useful at any age level. Frequently, even the most hesitant speaker (no matter what his/her age) can learn to relax and talk when hidden behind a puppet. If the puppet makes a mistake, it isn't nearly so bad as when the student makes a mistake. Thus a puppet takes the pressure off the student and places it on the puppet. You will find that your students will enjoy using puppets, and, if given time and encouragement, they will use them creatively.

HOW TO MAKE IT

1. Place the pattern on a folded piece of cloth. Cut out the pattern. You will get two cloth pieces like the pattern.

2. Sew the two pieces of cloth together along the dotted lines. Do not sew the bottom of the pieces together.

3. After sewing the two pieces of cloth together, turn the "glove" right side out, that is, with the seams inside.

Hint: the lower the eyes are placed the younger the face looks

4. Use cloth, buttons, ribbon, yarn and felt scraps to make the face.

5. A puppet is most effective when the person manipulating it is hidden from the audience. This can easily be achieved by placing a large box or poster paper on the desk. This enables the person manipulating the puppet to sit at the desk and not be seen.

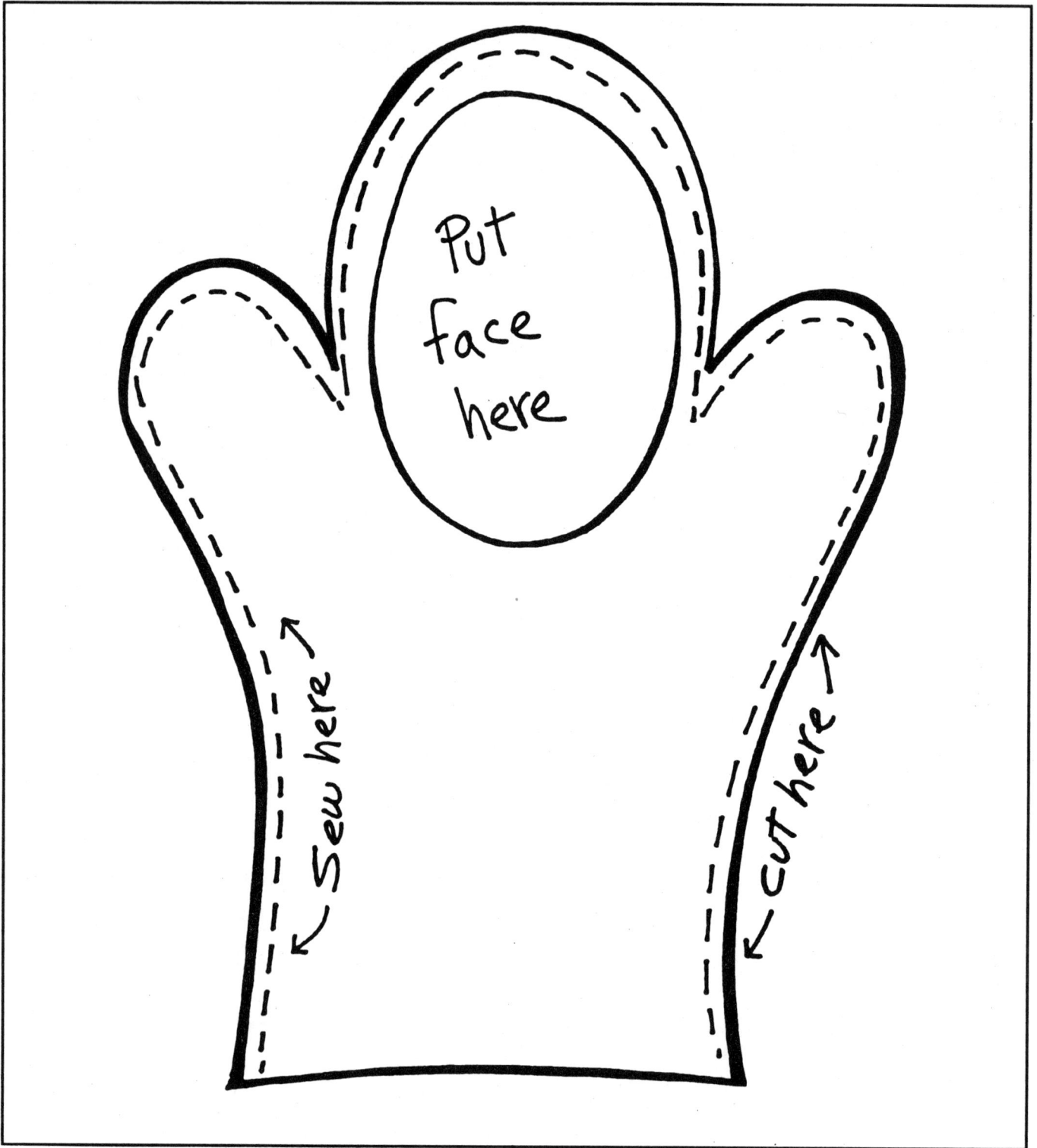

Put face here

Sew here →

cut here →

HOW TO USE IT

The teacher should be the first to demonstrate the use of puppets. Use them to introduce a lesson or as a review for a lesson. At this time the students are the observers and learn how a puppet can be manipulated. Later the students will use the puppets.

The first experience the students have with using the puppets should be in small groups or each student experimenting with a puppet. In this way the student can build self-confidence in speaking for the puppet and also in handling it.

Next, guide the students in creating dialogues for the puppets. Finally, the students should freely manipulate the puppets and use the structures, grammar and functions that they have already learned.

Teacher-led activity

Present tense

1. Put the puppet on your hand.
2. Have the puppet introduce himself/herself to the class.
3. Have the students ask the puppet basic information questions.
4. Have the puppet ask students basic information questions and give simple directions.

GLOVE PUPPETS

Example:

"What's your name?"   "How many brothers and sisters do you have?"
"Introduce me to the person sitting on your left."

5. Use the puppet to have the class use these functions:

    a. Introducing oneself and presenting others.
    b. Asking for basic information.
    c. Giving information about oneself.
    d. Asking and following directions.
    e. Giving directions.

Future tense

1. Three or four students get together and make a short presentation using the puppets.

2. They tell the audience what they are going to do, using as many "going to" structures as possible.

3. One possibility is to write a song using the "going to" structure.

Hint:
Give them
a well-known tune
to put words to.

Past tense

1. Have a group of three to five students make a short presentation with their puppets, using sentences in the past tense.

2. Have one of the puppets ask the class questions about the presentation to check their listening comprehension.

GLOVE PUPPETS

Example:

    a.   Who slept late last Saturday?
    b.   Did Alice play tennis last Thursday?
    c.   Did Albert go to the movies last Saturday night?

Grammar Explanation

1. Make a special puppet that can be used only for grammar explanations.
2. Use the puppet to introduce the lesson or to do a grammar review.
3. Have the puppet ask the students questions to keep their attention.
4. Have the students ask the puppet questions about the structure to check their understanding.

Grammar review

1. Have a group of three to five students prepare and present a grammar review on a specific structure.
2. Tell them to include the grammar points and example sentences.
3. Ask them to make their presentation as original and creative as possible.

13

STICK FIGURES

Explanation

Most of the units in this book contain instructions for making a particular visual aid and different uses for it. This unit, however, is not for a particular visual aid but rather gives instructions for making stick figures that can be used on many of your posters, on the blackboard, for illustrating handouts and exams, etc. There are several advantages to using stick figures in language teaching:

1. They are easy to make.

2. They are easy to replace if torn or lost.

3. They represent the specific action or idea that you need.

4. They can be drawn quickly and used effectively on the blackboard.

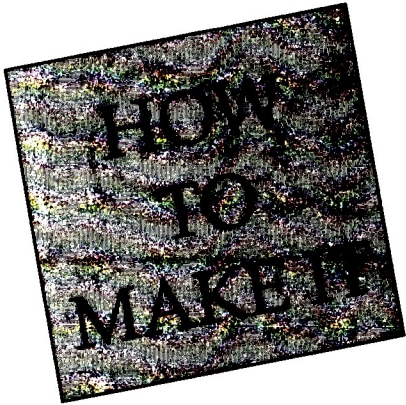

MALE FIGURE

1. Draw a circle for the head. Add facial features.

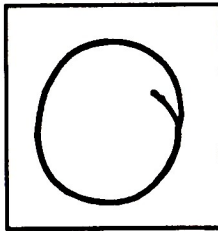

2. Draw a line for the body. Add arms and legs.

FEMALE FIGURE

1. Draw a circle for the head.

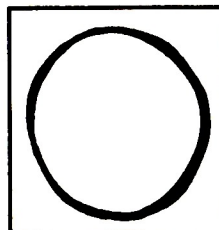

STICK FIGURES

Add facial features and hair.

2. Draw a triangle to represent the dress. Add arms and legs.

RUNNING

falling

SINGING

eating

To illustrate movement in the stick figure concentrate on the elbows, knees, and the position of the head.

HINT: Look at yourself in the mirror or ask a friend to pose for you. Look at the position of the knees, elbows and head. PRACTICE!

Add simple objects, labels, clothes, etc. to your stick figures in order to individualize them. For example, a cowboy hat and a star for a badge can make a stick figure into a sheriff. Add a label and he is in the Old West.

Start with the basic figure.
Add a label and a bag. She is a doctor.

Or add a label and a cap and she is a nurse.

We have used the signs and symbols shown on the following pages to individualize our stick figures.

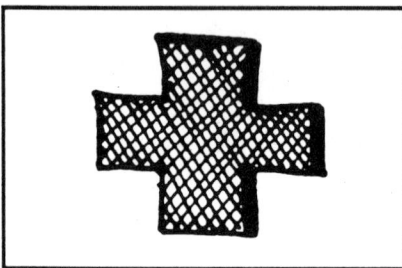

with the doctor or nurse

with the receptionist, secretary, businessman, or businesswoman

with the waiter, waitress, or cook

with the tennis players

with the bank teller, cashier, rich person

with the druggist

with the band, singer, musician, or radio

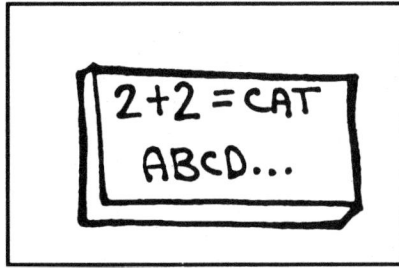

with the teacher or student

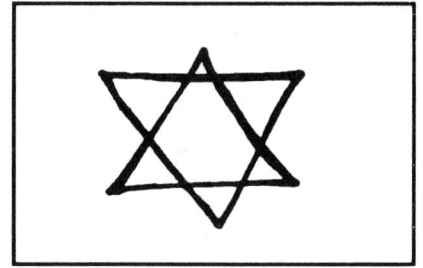

with the rabbi

with the priest or nun

with the entertainer, showgirl, or bartender

with the cowboy, cowgirl, showgirl, or bartender

with the college student

with the university professor

with the vacationers

STICK FIGURES

with the gambler, card player

with the sailor

with the queen and/or king

with a person thinking

with a person sleeping

with an angry person

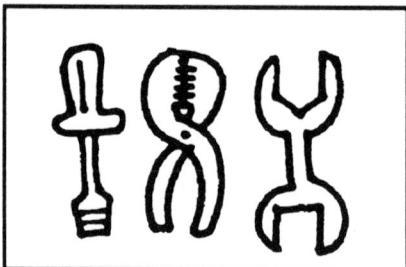

with the mechanic

with the carpenter

with the person who has a bright idea

10 CAN - CAN'T POSTER CARDS

CAN   CAN'T   CAN   CAN'T

CAN   CAN'T   CAN   CAN'T

CAN   CAN'T   CAN   CAN'T

CAN   CAN'T   CAN   CAN'T

I study English every day.

I'm Are.... do...does sometimes

Explanation

This visual is made up of pairs of cards that are used to demonstrate the use of the auxiliaries **CAN** and **CAN'T**. In each pair of cards, one card shows a picture or drawing of a person who **CAN** do an activity, and the other card shows a person who **CANNOT** do the activity. The students will immediately understand the pictures, and with explanation and examples, they will quickly understand how to use **CAN** and **CAN'T**.

CAN - CAN'T POSTER CARDS

HOW TO MAKE IT

1. On a piece of poster paper draw a simple stick figure doing an activity.

2. Draw another stick figure that obviously cannot do the activity.

Possible pairs:

CAN	CAN'T
a person running	a person wearing a cast
a person cooking	a person burning food
a person bullfighting	a person being gored
a person dancing	a person stepping on his/her partner's toes

3. Make several pairs of visuals with one card showing a person who CAN do the activity, and the other showing a person who CAN'T do the same activity.

HOW TO USE IT

Teacher-led activity

1. Show a visual with a person doing an activity. Give the students a sentence with **CAN**.

2. Show the other visual of a person who obviously **CAN'T** do the activity. Give an example with **CAN'T**.

3. Show a different visual with a person doing an activity. Ask students to make sentences with **CAN**.

4. Now show the visual with a person who is not able to do the activity. Ask for examples with **CAN'T**.

5. When you think the students have practiced this structure enough, have them practice making questions with **CAN**.

Group work

Student 1:	(gives information)	"Ernie can speak English."
Student 2:	(asks for information not shown on the visual)	"Can he speak Spanish, too?"
Student 1:	(answers question)	"Not a word!"

Give each student a different visual. The students ask each other questions about the visuals.

Example:

Student 1:   "John can't skate, but can he dance?"
Student 2:   "Yes, he can dance. He also plays the guitar, but he can't sing very well."

CAN - CAN'T POSTER CARDS

Open-ended exercise

Student 1:   "Can you _____ ?"

Student 2:   "Yes, I can." OR "No, I can't. Can you _____ ?"

Student 1:   "Yes, I can." OR "No, I can't, but I can _____ .
                    I like to _____ "

Student 2:   "I can _____ . _____ . When do you _____ ?"

Student 1:   " _____ . _____ ."

15 PREPOSITIONS

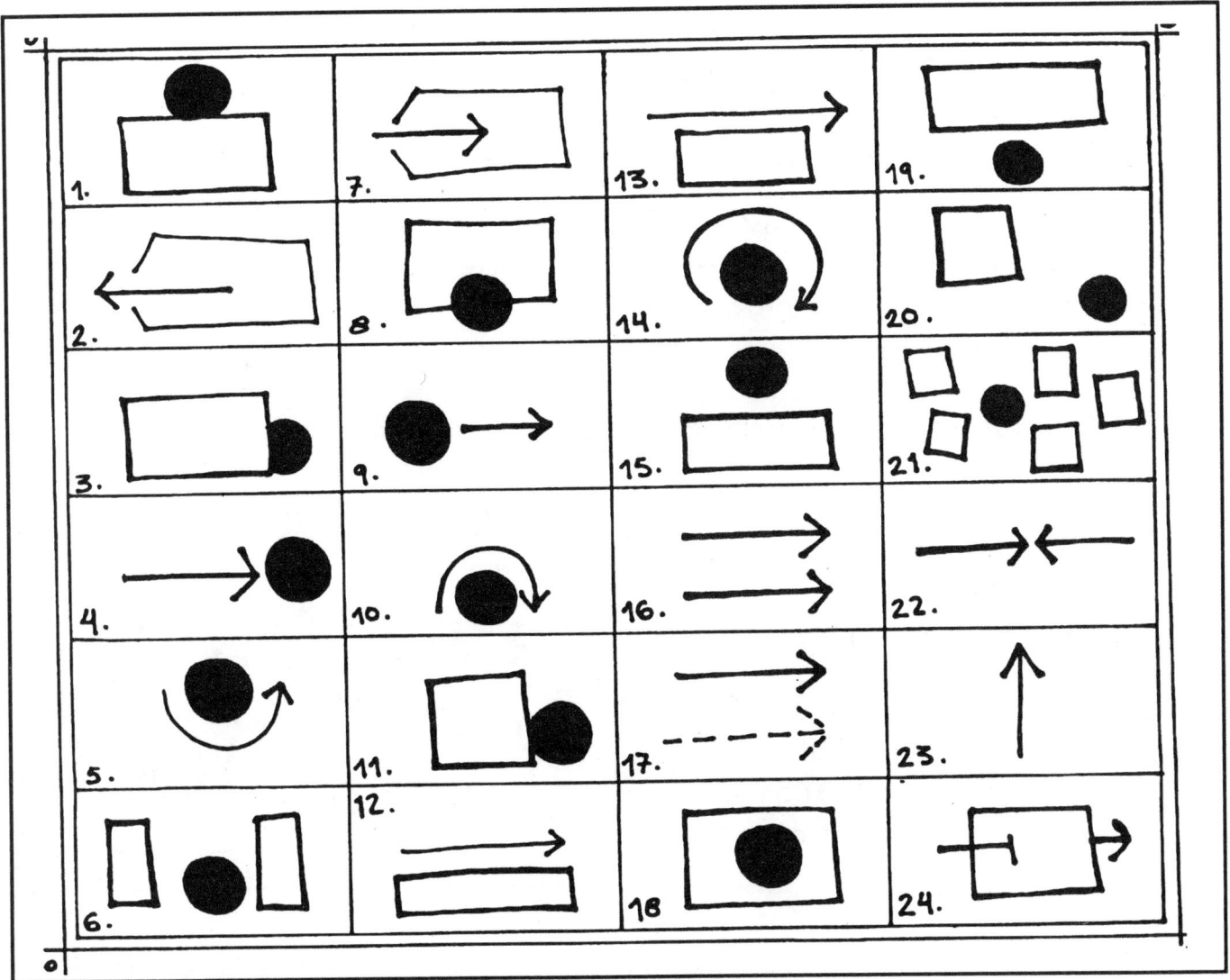

Explanation

This is a fun visual that is probably best used as a follow-up exercise to the study of prepositions. Present this visual after your students have a basic understanding of prepositions and their use, especially IN, ON, AT, FROM, NEAR, and TO. This activity lends itself to the use of the dictionary, writing and conversation.

HOW TO MAKE IT

1. Divide the poster paper into twenty-four equal parts. Several pieces of poster paper could be used for large groups.

2. Outline the sections with ink or plastic tape. Do not number the sections.

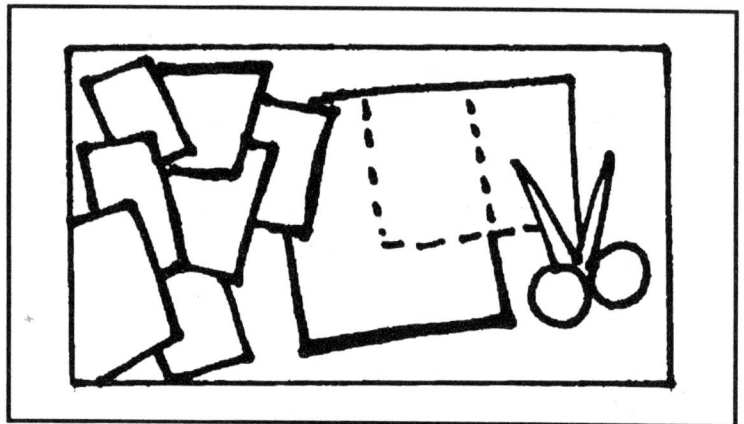

3. On a separate piece of paper (maybe a different color) cut twenty-four pieces that are slightly smaller than the sections on the poster paper.

4. On the pieces of paper that were cut in Step 3 draw the symbols, a different symbol for each of the twenty-four pieces.

5. These symbols are to be placed on the poster paper and attached with the plastic tape.

6. After Step 5 is completed, write the definition of the symbol on the poster paper, being careful to keep the entire word under the top flap.

HOW TO USE IT

Teacher-led activity

HINT:
For this visual each student or small group should have a dictionary. If you cannot supply the dictionaries ask your students to bring their own.

RESTAURANT
SIGN

SYMBOL

1. Explain the difference between:

2. Show them the visual, being careful not to reveal the words underneath. Give an example: "The ball is on the box."

3. Lift the flap to show the word ON.

Group work

1. When everyone understands the idea of the visual, divide the class into small groups and ask them to decide on a preposition that best defines each symbol.

2. After they have worked for a while, ask them to tell you the difference between OVER, UNDER, ABOVE, BELOW and AROUND.

3. Have each group write sentences using each of the prepositions illustrated.

4. Ask a student to point out the symbol for which he/she has written a sentence. Have this student write his/her sentence on the blackboard. Check the preposition by lifting the flap of the symbol the student indicated. Repeat this procedure with several students.

KEY

1.	ON	The ball is **on** the box.
2.	OUT OF	The arrow is going **out of** the box.
3.	BEHIND	The ball is **behind** the box.
4.	TO	The arrow is going **to** the target.
5.	UNDER	Water runs **under** the bridge.
6.	BETWEEN	The park is **between** First Street and Fifth Avenue.
7.	INTO	We go **into** the classroom at three o'clock.
8.	IN FRONT OF	John sits **in front of** the teacher's desk.
9.	FROM	The letter is **from** Alice.
10.	OVER	The plane flies **over** the mountain.
11.	AGAINST	The car is **against** the curb.
12.	ALONG	I walk **along** the river.
13.	BY	I walk **by** the store when I come to school.
14.	AROUND	The ring is **around** my finger.
15.	ABOVE	The picture is **above** the sofa.
16.	WITH	I go to the movies **with** my friend.

17.	WITHOUT	I drink coffee **without** sugar.
18.	IN	The ball is **in** the box.
19.	BELOW	The subway is **below** the street.
20.	NEAR	The school is **near** the park.
21.	AMONG	You are **among** friends.
22.	AGAINST	Mary is playing chess **against** Susan.
23.	UP	The boat goes **up** the river.
24.	THROUGH	The cat walked **through** the kitchen.

my
1

his
your
2

her
your
3

our
4

their
your
5

Explanation

This visual will help you teach the possessive adjectives: MY, YOUR, HIS, HER, OUR, ITS, and THEIR. It can be made on poster paper or drawn on the blackboard.

1. MY

Draw any character, male, female, or animal. (For suggestions on how to make stick figures, see Visual Number 13.)

Make one arm noticeably longer than the other. Draw the hand of this arm in the shape of an arrow and have the arrow pointing to the figure itself, signifying **MY**.

Character 1

2. YOUR/HIS/HER

Draw any character, male, female, or animal; this time draw the hand pointing away from the character.

Character 2   Character 3

Character 4

3. **OUR**
Draw two or more characters together, with one hand of each character pointing back to the characters.

Character 5

4. **THEIR/YOUR**
Draw a character as in Step 2 with the hand pointing away from the character. This character would say YOUR or THEIR.

MY, YOUR, HIS, HER, OUR, ITS, THEIR

5. In addition to the figures you will need various objects that the characters will possess. A variety of things can be used:

a. Use objects that you have in the classroom:
pencils, books, chalk, notebooks.

b. Use objects that you and your students may have with you:
money, wallet, briefcase, umbrella, purse.

c. Use the things you may have as teaching aids:
magazines, toys, pictures, flash cards.

HOW TO USE IT

1. Place or draw the first visual on the blackboard.

2. Place one of the objects beside the character. Be careful not to cover the arrow.

3. Say what character 1 would say, for example, "This is MY magazine."

4. Place the second figure on the blackboard with the arrow pointing toward character 1.

5. Say what character 2 would say, for example, "That's YOUR magazine."

MY, YOUR, HIS, HER, OUR, ITS, THEIR

Draw a line from the second character's eyes to the eyes of the first character and explain that we use YOUR when we are talking about the person or animal we are speaking to. Give several examples using students and their belongings in order to demonstrate the use of YOUR. Remember to look only at the student you are talking to.

6. Erase the chalk lines you have drawn from the first to the second character's eyes.

7. Tell the class that character 2 is looking and talking to the class. Have character 2 talk about character 1 and say that it is **ITS/HIS/HER** magazine. Practice this with the class using students' belongings to practice "This is **HIS/HER** pen, pencil, notebook, etc." Be sure not to look at the student you are talking about although you are pointing at him/her.

8. Show or draw the third visual on the blackboard. If the second visual was a girl then this one should be a boy, so you can practice **HIS/HER**. Repeat the same process as in numbers 5, 6, and 7.

9. Show or draw the fourth visual. This one should be the plural (two animals or people). Repeat the same process as in numbers 5 through 7.

10. Move the object from visual to visual, having the class practice **MY, YOUR, HIS,** and **HER.**

11. Put the object on the plural visual and tell the class that they, the students, are talking. Have the class respond "It's **OUR** _____ (object)." Practice by moving the object around from visual to visual to give the clue to the students about who is talking.

MY, YOUR, HIS, HER, OUR, ITS, THEIR

Example:

    A.   Teacher puts the object on character 1.
Have the students respond "This is **MY** _____ ."

    B.   Leave the object on character 1. Tell the class that character 4 is talking and looking at the class.
Have the class respond "It's **HIS** _____ ."

    C.   Tell the class that character 4 is looking at character 1.
Have the class respond "It's **YOUR** _____ ."

12. Repeat A, B, C for all the different visuals so all the possessives are practiced.

13. Follow up this activity with students from your class. Be sure to have them look at the class and point to someone to practice **HIS**, **HER**, or **THEIR**. Have them look directly at individual students or pairs to practice **YOUR**. Have them point to themselves while holding the object to say **MY**.

NOTE: This seems like a complicated explanation for possessive adjectives, but the student will grasp the idea and be able to manipulate the figures and objects very quickly. Remember, you must be in control of the situation and give clear instructions and illustrations at the beginning. Be patient!

Explanation

Although this visual has many uses we like it best for working with the comparative and superlative forms of adjectives and adverbs. This is often a difficult structure to practice, so students will appreciate a visual that is fun and easy to understand. Students will look at

COMPARISONS

the visual and see the similarities and differences between two people, places or objects. They will also have the opportunity to use all the forms of the comparative:

more _____ than   as _____ as

_____ er than   as _____ a _____ as

When these forms have been practiced sufficiently, unfold the visual so that three people, places or objects are visible. Now the students can use the superlative to compare and contrast the three things they see. They will be able to use:

the most   and   the _____est

This visual can also be used in beginning classes for description.

HOW
TO
MAKE IT

1. Tape three poster papers together.

2. Select three pictures to be used for the visual. We've chosen children with pets. Other possibilities are CARS, HOUSES, ANIMALS, ATHLETES, JEWELRY, CLOTHING, BEACH, RESORTS.

3. Draw or find pictures of two subjects that are the same in some respects, but different in others. Ours are twins. Other possibilities are two athletes who are the same height, weight or age; two cars that are the same price or have the same size engine.

4. Draw the third subject, making sure that it differs in many aspects from the other two.

COMPARISONS

HOW TO USE IT

1. Unfold the visual so that the two people, objects, or places can be seen.

2. Give the students examples using comparatives. Example: "Sue has longer hair than John." Practice the following structures:

a.   John is **more** intelligent **than** Sue.

b.   John is **as** good a student **as** Sue.

c.   Sue is **as** old **as** John.

HINT: Present one form of the comparative in one lesson. Give your students the opportunity to practice this form before presenting the other forms.

3. Ask students for more examples of the form of the comparative you are practicing.

4. After students have had plenty of practice using the comparative forms, unfold the third panel so that all three subjects are visible.

5. Give the students examples using the superlative.

Example:

a. Mary is **the** young**est** in the family.

b. Sue is **the most** interesting of the three.

6. Ask students to give more examples.

Group exercise

Student 1: (Gives information)
"Sue is taller than John."

Student 2: (Asks question)
"Is she older than John?"

Student 3: (Answers question)
"No, she isn't. She's the youngest in the family."

COMPARISONS

Open-ended exercise

Student 1:   "Is _____ faster than _____?"

Student 2:   "Yes, _____ is, but _____ is

_____ er than _____."

Student 1:   "Is _____ the _____est in the

_____?"

Student 2:   "No, I think _____ is the _____est.

_____?"

Student 1:   "_____. _____."

Explanation

This color-coded chart is a versatile and entertaining visual. Each family member is given a color that corresponds to his daily activities throughout the week. The chart provides a guide for talking about the family members, using various grammatical structures.

COLOR-CODED CHART

HOW TO MAKE IT

1. Tape two large pieces of poster paper together. Put tape on both sides of the joint.

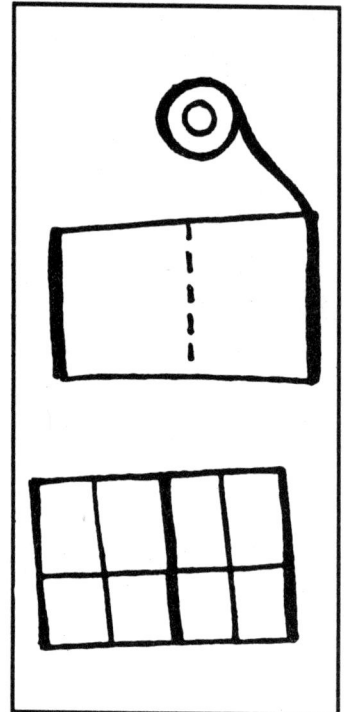

2. Divide the paper into eight equal sections. This gives the first section for the family and the seven remaining sections for the days of the week.

HINT: Divide the paper with colored tape. This adds color as well as strength.

3. Put a four-member family (only four) in the first section with simple clear figures. Use simple stick figures, drawn with a black marker.

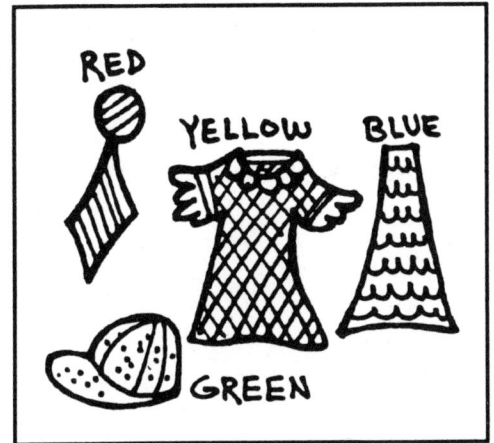
RED
YELLOW
BLUE
GREEN

4. Each member is identified by a color. For example: Father's tie is red. Mother's dress is blue. These are the only four colors used in the poster.

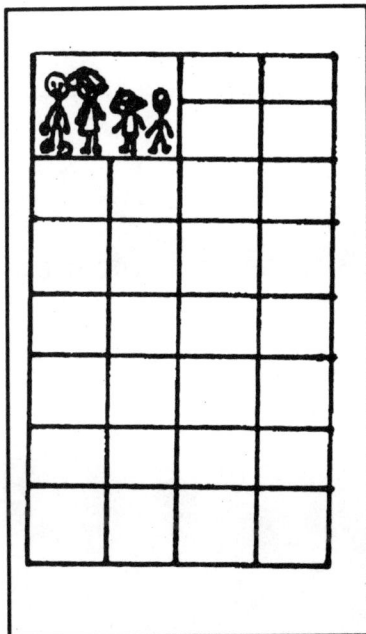

5. Divide each of the seven remaining squares, which represent the days of the week, into four equal sections. Each day has four sections; color one section of each day with one of the family member's colors.

Example: Father's tie is red, so one section of each day of the week will be red. Mother's dress is blue, so one section of all seven parts will be blue. This will identify the family member who is doing the activity placed on his/her color.

When this is finished, all seven days of the week will be divided into the four colors corresponding to the family members.

MONDAY
TUESDAY
WEDNESDAY

6. Label the seven sections with the days of the week. Use a black marker.

7. Make simple black and white drawings representing activities that the family might do during the week. Make these big enough to be easily seen but small enough to fit into the colored section leaving some of the color visible. Think of activities that can be done by individuals and also some activities that can be shared by two or more family members.

a. Bicycle   d. Church
b. The wash e. Baseball
c. Cards

Some activities would be more easily understood by using words rather than pictures.
Example:

a. Jogging   d. Judo
b. Office   e. Meditation
c. Restaurant

8. On the back of each activity staple a small piece of Velcro. Another piece of Velcro is stapled in the middle of each colored square. Also staple a small piece of Velcro where the four colors intersect. This will allow shared activities to be shown.

HOW TO USE IT

GENERAL INFORMATION FOR ALL STRUCTURES

Explain the color coding to the students: Father's tie is red, this section is red; therefore, any activity placed in this section is done by the father. Any activity that overlaps two or more colors is a shared activity.

Example: RESTAURANT is on blue and red on Saturday so the mother and the father go to a restaurant on Saturday.

All the activities are detachable so any family member can be given any activity.

The following instructions will give you ideas on how to practice several verb tenses. Begin with the **Teacher-led activity**. After the students have practiced simple sentences with the appropriate tense, have them practice forming questions. Follow the **Teacher-led activity** with **Group work** or the **Open-ended exercise**.

SATURDAY
RESTAURANT

Structure - SIMPLE PRESENT TENSE

Teacher-led activity

1. Take a drawing of an activity, for example, racquetball. Place the drawing in Mrs. Smith's section of the square for Tuesday.

2. Give an example: "Mrs. Smith plays racquetball on Tuesdays."

3. Elicit examples from the students, using different activities by placing different activity cards in different family members' sections.

COLOR-CODED CHARTS

Group work

Student 1:   (Gives information)
"Mrs. Smith plays racquetball on Tuesdays."

Student 2:   (Asks question)
"Does Mr. Smith play racquetball on Tuesdays too?"

Student 3:   (Answers the question by looking at the visual)
"No, he doesn't. He jogs on Tuesdays."

Open-ended exercise

Student 1:   "Do you play racquetball on Tuesdays?"

Student 2:   "Yes, I do." OR "No, I don't. I usually _____ on Tuesdays. Do you like racquetball?"

Student 1:   "Yes, I do." OR "No, I don't. I _____ ."

Student 2:   "Do you _____ ?"

Student 1:   "_____ . _____ ."

Student 2:   "What day do you _____?"

Student 1:   "I _____ ."

Structure - SIMPLE PAST TENSE

Teacher-led activity

1. Point to the appropriate square representing the actual day of the week. "Today is Thursday."

2. Explain that any activity done by the family before today is in the past, so the simple past is used.

3. Take a drawing of an activity, for example, "church." Place it at the intersection of the four colors in the square for Sunday.

4. Give an example: "The Smith family went to church last Sunday."

5. Elicit examples from the students, using different activities and placing them in the appropriate family members' sections.

Group work

Student 1: (Gives information)
"The Smith family ate at a restaurant last Sunday."
Student 2: (Asks question)
"Did they go to the movies after they ate out?"
Student 3: (Answers question by looking at the visual.)
"No, they didn't. They went to a concert."

Open-ended exercise

Student 1: "Did you go to a concert last Sunday?"
Student 2: "No, I didn't. I went_____. What did you do?"
Student 1: "I _____. _____."
Student 2: "_____."

Structure - PRESENT CONTINUOUS TENSE

Teacher-led activity

1. Point to the appropriate square representing the actual day of the week. "Today is Monday."

2. Take a drawing representing an activity, for example, "ballet." Place the drawing in Mary's section of the square.

3. Give an example: "Mary is taking ballet lessons today."

COLOR-CODED CHART

4. Elicit examples from the students using the activities of the other family members.

Group work

Student 1: (Gives information)
"Mary is taking ballet lessons today."
Student 2: (Asks a question)
"Is Billy playing baseball today?"
Student 3: (Answers the question by looking at the visual.)
"No, he isn't. He's bicycling today."

Open-ended exercise

Student 1: "What are you doing today?"
Student 2: "I'm _____ today. What are you doing?"
Student 1: "I'm _____ because I _____ ."

Structure - PAST CONTINUOUS TENSE

Teacher-led activity

1. Point to the appropriate square representing the actual day of the week. "Today is Saturday."

2. Explain that any activity done by the family before today is in the past. If two activities occurred at the same time in the past, the past continuous may be used.

3. Take two drawings representing two different activities and place them in the appropriate family members' sections.

4. Give an example: "Billy was playing baseball while Mary was swimming."

5. Elicit examples from the students, using different activities and placing them in the appropriate family members' sections.

Group work

Student 1: (Gives information)
"Billy played baseball last Saturday."
Student 2: (Asks question)
"What was Mary doing while he was playing baseball?"
Student 3: (Answers question by looking at the visual)
"She was swimming while he was playing baseball."

Open-ended exercise

Student 1: "What were you doing while I was jogging yesterday?"
Student 2: "What time were you jogging?"
Student 1: "At 6:00 p.m."
Student 2: "I was _____ **ing** while you were jogging."
Student 1: "I was _____ **ing** while you were_____**ing**."

Structure - PRESENT PERFECT TENSE

Teacher-led exercise

1. Explain that today is Thursday. Point to Thursday on the visual.

2. Explain that any activity done from Monday to Thursday is past tense or an activity that has already been done.

3. Explain that any activity done from Thursday to Sunday is future tense or an activity that hasn't yet been done. For example, point to the square for Tuesday showing the drawing of the guitar in Billy's section: "Billy has already taken his guitar lesson this week." Point to the square for Friday and the drawing representing Judo in Mary's section: "Mary hasn't gone to her Judo class yet this week."

Group work

Student 1:   "Has Mr. Smith gone to the market?"

Student 2:   "No, he hasn't gone yet. He's going to go after lunch." OR "Yes, he's already gone to the market."

Open-ended exercise

Student 1:   "Have you written your report yet?"

Student 2:   "Yes, I have, but I haven't ——————————— yet.
Have you ——————————— ?"

Student 1:   "————— , ————— . ——————————— . ——————————— ."
——————————— ?"

Student 2:   "————— , ——————————————————————————— ."

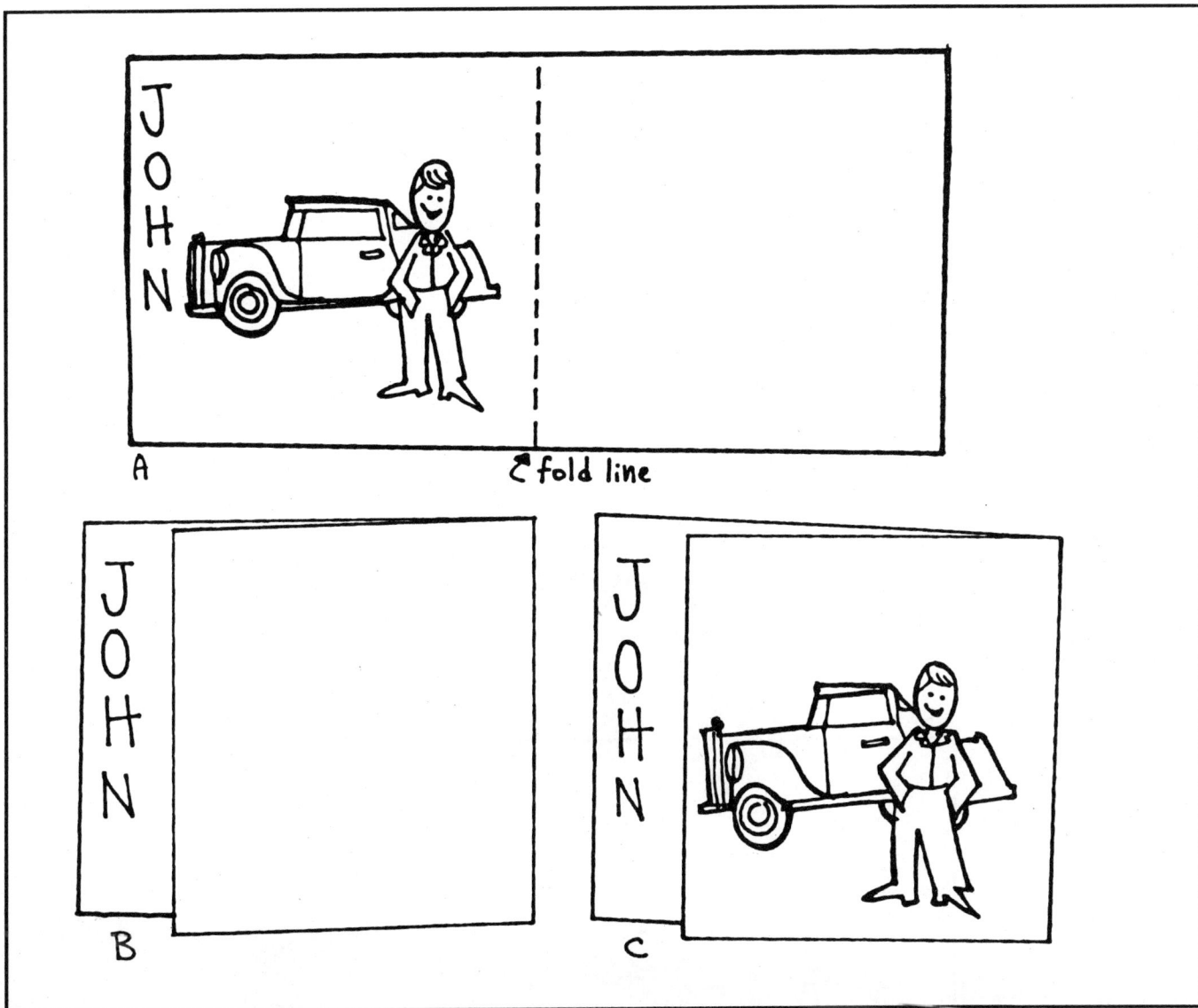

A

↙ fold line

B

C

Explanation

This visual provides a useful open-ended approach to teaching USED TO, STILL, ANYMORE with present and past tenses. It is also useful at beginning levels to practice questions with DO and DOES. It can also be used to practice the PRESENT PERFECT CONTINUOUS.

HOW TO USE IT

1. Select two related magazine pictures.

   Example: A man beside a big car and a second picture of a man beside a small car.

2. Glue one picture on the front side of a rectangular piece of poster paper. The size of the poster paper will depend on the size of your class and the size of the pictures used. The visual should be big enough to be seen and understood by the entire group, but small enough to be manageable in groups of three to six.

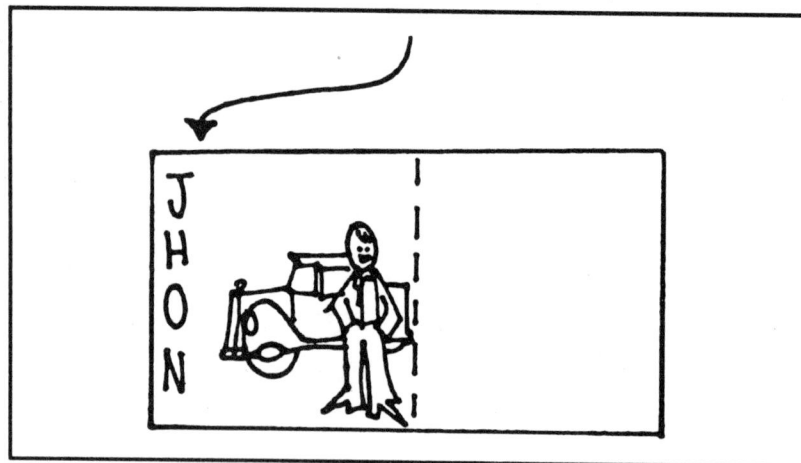

3. Write the title or key words in the space to the left of the first picture.

4. Fold the paper to cover the first picture but not the title. The title will indicate to the viewer that both pictures represent the same person or people. This needs to be done because it is difficult to find two or more magazine pictures with the same people.

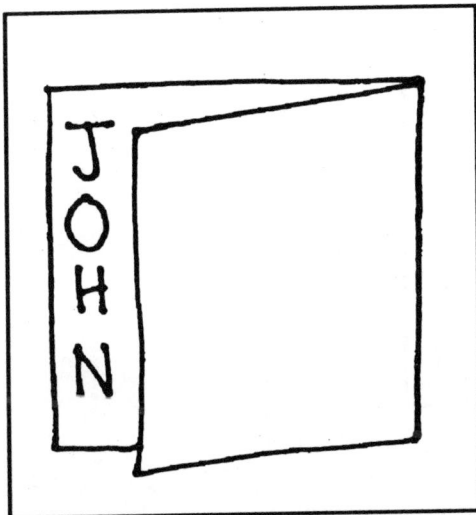

5. With the paper folded and the title showing, glue the second picture on the overlapping sheet.

6. Tape the edges with the plastic tape.

7. Make several different sets of visuals using different ideas so the structure can be learned by the group as a whole and practiced in small groups.

FLIP CARDS

Possible ideas:

> a. Two different sports:
>   football/basketball
>   tennis/golf
>   racquetball/baseball
>
> b. Two different cars:
>   different makes
>   different colors
>
> c. Two different hair colors:
>   blond/brunette
>   redhead/gray
>
> d. Two different television sets:
>   portable/console
>
> e. Two different perfumes:
>   Arpege/Chanel

8. If you cannot find the exact picture you want to illustrate your idea, for example, a man beside a new Ford, cut out a new Ford from a magazine advertisement and combine the two pictures to make one visual.

HOW
TO
USE IT

GENERAL INFORMATION FOR ALL STRUCTURES

Teacher-led activity

Use a variety of visuals and elicit appropriate examples from the entire class or from individuals.

Individual work

Each student gives his response to each visual orally or in writing.

Group work

The class is divided into groups. Each group has a visual to practice the structure using the basic format (see below). The visuals are exchanged between groups, allowing each group to practice with a variety of visuals.

Open-ended exercise

After practicing several different examples using any of the methods listed above, have a student ask his/her classmates original questions.

Examples:

"Do you _____ ?"
"Does your brother _____ ?"
"Do you and your family _____ ?"
"Does your teacher _____ ?"

These questions could be taken from the visuals or from words listed by the teacher on the blackboard.

Examples:

1.	new car	6.	eat pizza
2.	Dallas	7.	paint
3.	swimming	8.	ride a horse
4.	play golf	9.	Los Angeles
5.	bowl		

Students should give true answers. At this point any logical answer is acceptable because the students are giving personal information. Remember, the idea is to move from the pattern practice of the different visuals to a real situation with the students talking about themselves. When the topic is exhausted, the students begin with another question based on the visuals or ask an original question that will lead to another short exchange of ideas.

Structure - USED TO, STILL, ANYMORE

Teacher-led activity

1. Hold the open visual before the class showing Picture 1 and the title "John."

2. Give an example such as: "John used to drive a big car."

3. Fold the visual, covering Picture 1 while showing Picture 2. Given another example such as: "John doesn't have a Ford anymore. Now he has a Volkswagen."

4. Ask students to produce questions with **USED TO**, using the same visual or a different one. Have other students answer these questions with **STILL** or **ANYMORE**.

5. Have the students practice the structure using different visuals.

6. Have the students follow up the practice with the open- ended exercise.

Group work

Student 1: (Gives information)
"John used to drive an LTD."

Student 2: (Asks a question using STILL)
"Does he still drive an LTD?"

Student 3: (Answers the question by showing either Picture 1 or Picture 2 and gives the correct response.)
"Yes, he still drives an LTD." OR "No, he doesn't drive an LTD anymore. Now he drives a Volkswagen."

Open-ended exercise

Student 1:   "Did you use to have an LTD?"
Student 2:   "No, I didn't. I used to have a motorcycle."
Student 1:   "Do you still have a motorcycle?"
Student 2:   "No, I don't, but my cousin does. We go to the country every weekend."
Student 1:   "What do you do in the country?"
Student 2:   "We _____ ."
Student 1:   "Did you use to _____?"
Student 2:   " _____ ."
Student 1:   "Do you still _____?"
Student 2:   " _____ ."

Structure - DO, DOES

Teacher-led activity

1. Hold the open visual before the class showing Picture 1 and the title "John."

2. Ask a question such as: "Does John have a big car?"

3. Fold the visual, covering Picture 1 and showing Picture 2. Answer the question with an example such as: "No, he doesn't. He has a Volkswagen."

4. Elicit examples from the students using either the same visual or a different one.

5. Have the students practice the structure.

6. Have the students follow the practice with the open-ended exercise.

Group work

Have one student ask a question about the pictures. A second student should give a short answer and then give more information.

Example:

Student 1:   (Holding Picture 1)
              "Does John have an LTD?"
Student 2:   "No, he doesn't. He has a Volkswagen."

Open-ended exercise

Student 1:   "Do you have a Volkswagen?"

Student 2: "No, I don't. I don't have a car. I usually ride the bus. Do you ride the bus too?"

Student 1: "_____ , _____ . _____ ."

Structure - PRESENT PERFECT CONTINUOUS

Teacher-led activity

1. Hold the open visual before the class, showing Picture 1 and the title "John."

2. Give an example such as: "John has been driving a big car for several years."

3. Fold the visual, covering Picture 1 while showing Picture 2. Give another example such as: "John has been thinking about buying a smaller car."

4. Ask students to produce questions or sentences using the present perfect continuous structure. Show them a different visual.

5. Have the students follow up the practice with small group work or an open-ended exercise.

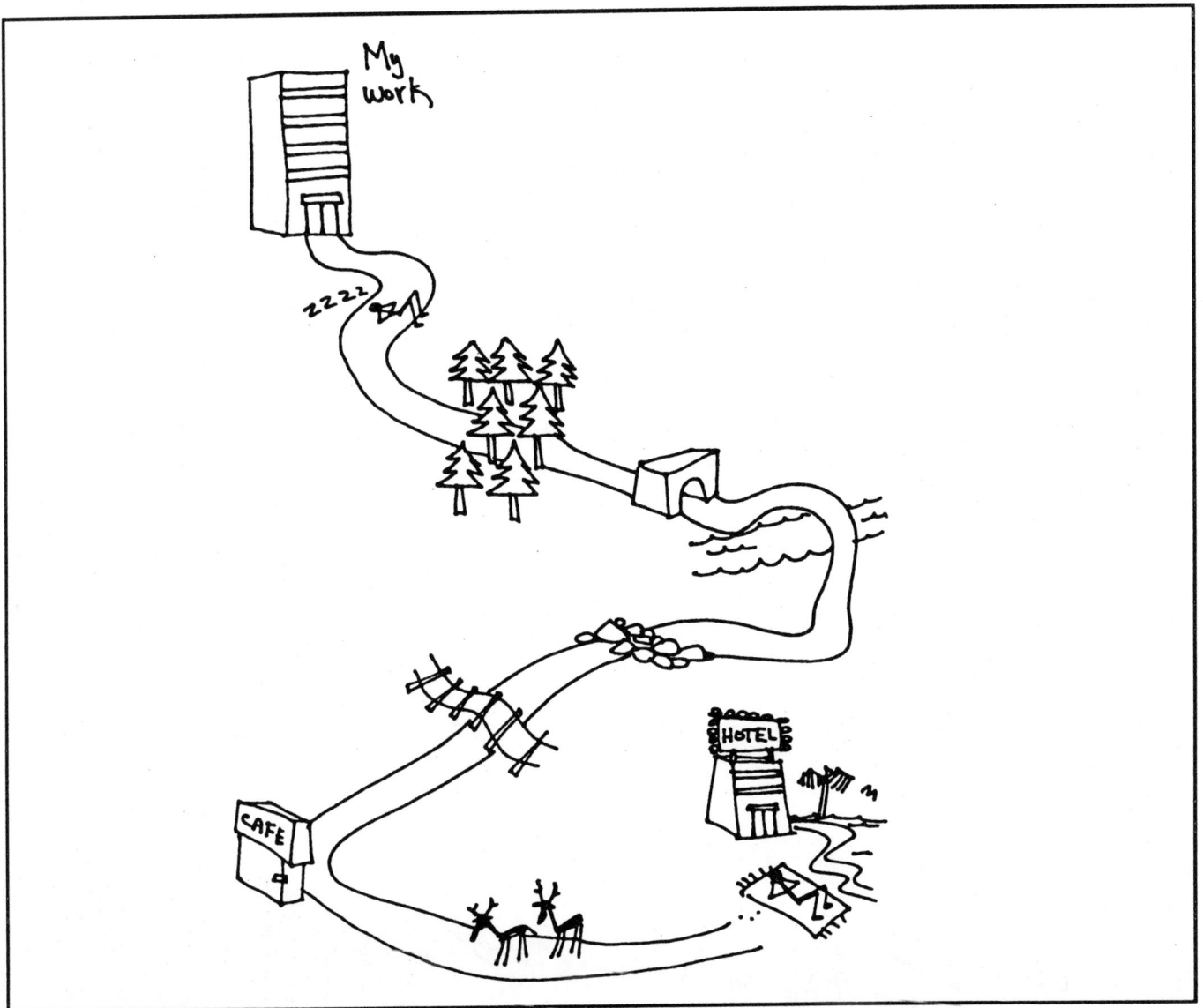

Explanation

This is perhaps one of the most flexible visuals of the book as it can be used with any level and to practice any grammatical structure or lexical area. It can be adapted to be used as a game to evaluate the students' understanding of a specific grammar point.

POSSIBILITY ONE

1. Take a large piece of poster paper and draw a long, winding road across it. Use several pieces of poster paper for large groups.

NOTE: This visual can also be drawn on the blackboard.

2. Draw a house at the beginning and end of the road and draw in several smaller houses along the way. The number of the houses you draw will depend on the size of your group.

3. Label the first house "My House" and the last house "The Party."

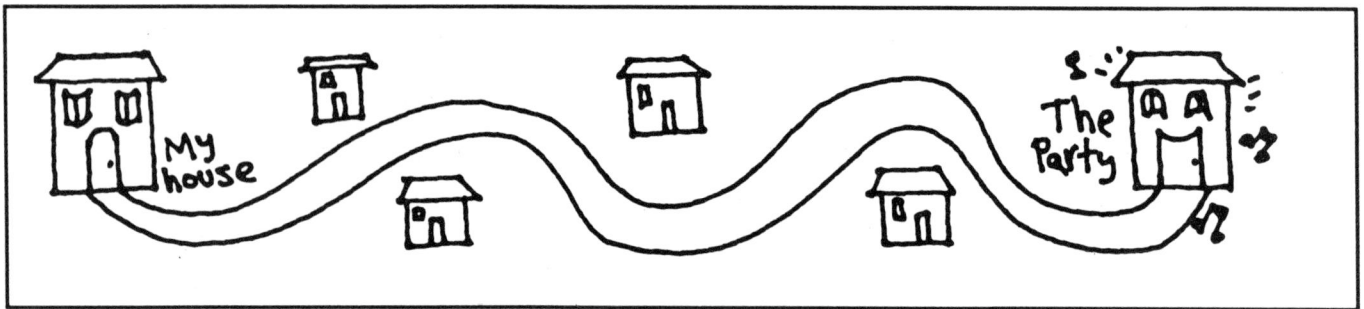

4. Cut out two pictures of vehicles from a magazine or draw and cut your own and place them outside "My House." If there are more than two teams competing, simply add more vehicles.

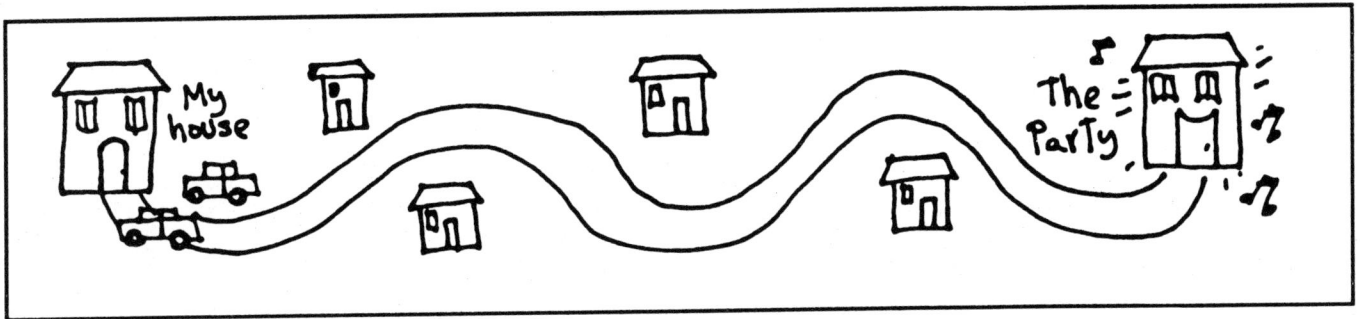

HOW TO USE IT

ANY GRAMMAR STRUCTURE.

The idea of the visual is to test the students' knowledge of the grammar and to see which team is the first to win the race.

1. Divide the group into teams.

2. Each team chooses a vehicle and places it at "My House."

3. Toss a coin to see which team starts.

4. The teacher asks a question related to the grammatical area being practiced. If the team answers correctly, their vehicle moves to the first house. The team will continue along the road until they fail to answer correctly.

5. If the teams are large, put the name of each team member into a hat and draw names to ensure everyone has a chance to participate.

ROAD RACE

There are various ways of asking the questions:

Example:

1. Simply ask the students to produce a sentence in a given tense and form.
2. Give the students an incorrect sentence and have them spot and correct the mistake.
   "I have been playing tennis since three hours."
3. Give the students a sentence with the verb in the infinitive. Have them put the verb in the correct tense.
   "Kate see her grandmother yesterday."
4. Provide the students with alternative answers to a question.
   "Did you go to the cinema with John?"
   a) Yes, I go with him every day.
   b) Yes, I did.
   c) Yes, I went with John yesterday.
5. Have your students transform a sentence from one tense into another.
   Put the following sentence into the passive tense.
   "We use trees to make paper."

HOW TO MAKE IT

POSSIBILITY TWO

1. As with the previous visual, draw a long, winding road across one or several pieces of poster paper.

2. Draw a large house at the beginning and at the end of the road and label them.
   Possible buildings to mark the beginning and end of the road are:
   a. dungeon and castle
   b. primary school and university
   c. office block and beachside hotel

3. Draw in various obstacles that you normally expect to find on a road. These may include a tunnel, a bridge, a river or a wood. The number of items you include will depend on the size of your group.

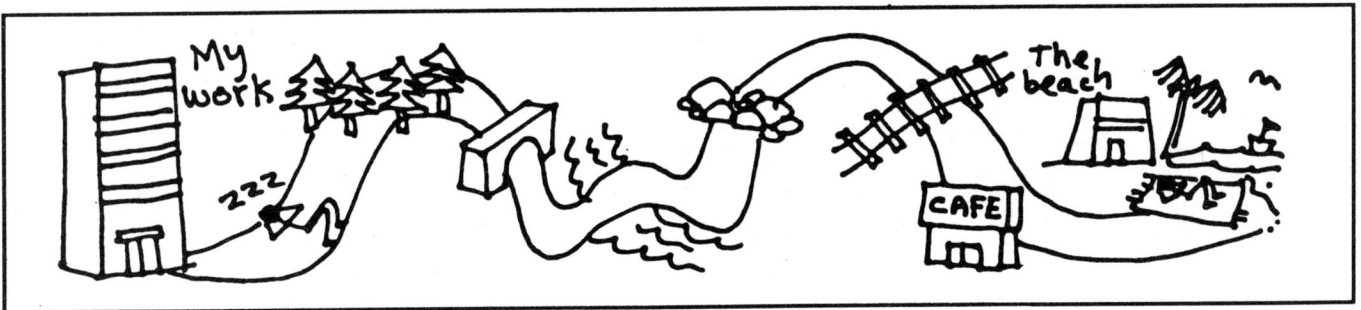

HOW
TO
USE IT

1. Divide the group into teams. Each team is represented by a different vehicle, all of which start at the first house.

2. In order to advance along the road, each team has to produce a sentence using a preposition to describe how they are overcoming the obstacles.

Example:

"We are going **past** the church."
"We are going **through** the tunnel."

You may have your students repeat each movement from the beginning to be sure they have understood the use of the prepositions.

NTC ESL/EFL TEXTS AND MATERIAL
Junior High—Adult Education

Computer Software
Amigo
Basic Vocabulary Builder on Computer

Language and Culture Readers
Beginner's English Reader
Advanced Beginner's English Reader
Cultural Encounters in the U.S.A.
Passport to America Series
  California Discovery
  Adventures in the Southwest
  The Coast-to-Coast Mystery
  The New York Connection
Discover America Series
  California, Chicago, Florida, Hawaii,
  New England, New York, Texas,
  Washington, D.C.
Looking at America Series
  Looking at American Signs, Looking at
  American Food, Looking at American
  Recreation, Looking at American Holidays
Time: We the People
Communicative American English
English á la Cartoon

Text/Audiocassette Learning Packages
Speak Up! Sing Out!
Listen and Say It Right in English!

Transparencies
Everyday Situations in English

**Duplicating Masters and
Black-line Masters**
The Complete ESL/EFL Cooperative and
  Communicative Activity Book
Easy Vocabulary Games
Vocabulary Games
Advanced Vocabulary Games
Play and Practice!
Basic Vocabulary Builder
Practical Vocabulary Builder
Beginning Activities for English
  Language Learners
Intermediate Activities for English
  Language Learners
Advanced Activities for English
  Language Learners

Language-Skills Texts
Starting English with a Smile
English with a Smile
More English with a Smile
English Survival Series
  Building Vocabulary, Recognizing Details,
  Identifying Main Ideas, Writing Sentences
  and Paragraphs, Using the Context
English Across the Curriculum
Essentials of Reading and Writing English
Everyday English
Everyday Situations for Communicating in
  English
Learning to Listen in English
Listening to Communicate in English
Communication Skillbooks
Living in the U.S.A.
Basic English Vocabulary Builder Activity Book
Basic Everyday Spelling Workbook
Practical Everyday Spelling Workbook

Advanced Readings and Communicative
  Activities for Oral Proficiency
Practical English Writing Skills
Express Yourself in Written English
Campus English
English Communication Skills for Professionals
Speak English!
Read English!
Write English!
Orientation in American English
Building English Sentences
Grammar for Use
Grammar Step-by-Step
Listening by Doing
Reading by Doing
Speaking by Doing
Vocabulary by Doing
Writing by Doing
Look, Think and Write

Life- and Work-Skills Texts
English for Success
Building Real Life English Skills
Everyday Consumer English
Book of Forms
Essential Life Skills series
Finding a Job in the United States
English for Adult Living
Living in English
Prevocational English

TOEFL and University Preparation
NTC's Preparation Course for the TOEFL®
NTC's Practice Tests for the TOEFL®
How to Apply to American Colleges
  and Universities
The International Student's Guide
  to the American University

Dictionaries and References
ABC's of Languages and Linguistics
Everyday American English Dictionary
Building Dictionary Skills in
  English (workbook)
Beginner's Dictionary of American
  English Usage
Beginner's English Dictionary
  Workbook
NTC's American Idioms Dictionary
NTC's Dictionary of American Slang
  and Colloquial Expressions
NTC's Dictionary of Phrasal Verbs
NTC's Dictionary of Grammar Terminology
Essential American Idioms
Contemporary American Slang
Forbidden American English
101 American English Idioms
101 American English Proverbs
Practical Idioms
Essentials of English Grammar
The Complete ESL/EFL Resource Book
Safari Grammar
Safari Punctuation
303 Dumb Spelling Mistakes
TESOL Professional Anthologies
  Grammar and Composition
  Listening, Speaking, and Reading
  Culture

For further information or a current catalog, write:
National Textbook Company
a division of *NTC Publishing Group*
4255 West Touhy Avenue
Lincolnwood, Illinois 60646-1975 U.S.A.